THE NATURE OF TRAUMA
IN AMERICAN NOVELS

MICHELLE BALAEV

THE Nature OF Trauma IN American NOVELS

NORTHWESTERN UNIVERSITY PRESS

EVANSTON, ILLINOIS

Northwestern University Press
www.nupress.northwestern.edu

Printed in the United States of America

10 9 8 7 6 5 4 3 2 1

Library of Congress Cataloging-in-Publication Data

Balaev, Michelle.
    The nature of trauma in American novels / Michelle Balaev.
      p. cm.
    Includes bibliographical references and index.
    ISBN 978-0-8101-2819-4 (cloth : alk. paper)—ISBN 978-0-8101-2820-0
(pbk. : alk. paper)
      1. American fiction—History and criticism. 2. Psychic trauma in literature.
3. Memory in literature. 4. Landscapes in literature. I. Title.
PS374.P69B35 2012
813'.5409353—dc23

2011041634

Dedicated to Misha

contents

Acknowledgments

Many people have been important to my ideas on this topic and have generously provided feedback and support. I benefited from thoughtful feedback by Mary Wood, who provided crucial critiques of the manuscript in its early stages. Scott Slovic has provided significant encouragement and a valuable dialogue on this project—a conversation with Scott over a decade ago started me down the path toward writing this book. Betsy Wheeler provided a careful reading of the manuscript that was essential to my thinking about the topic and the final form of the book. James S. Hans has provided enthusiastic support and keen insights on my work. Patti Fitchen, with her intellectual brilliance, creativity, and mentorship, encouraged me to trust my ideas and follow my ambitions. A conversation with Linda Lomperis, who taught a phenomenal course on feminist and queer theory at the University of California, Santa Cruz, provided the initial direction to pursue my ecocritical interests. Santa Cruz with its redwoods, meadows, Pacific coastline, and unique community was the perfect place to ground me before beginning this work. Henry L. Carrigan Jr. at Northwestern University Press generously provided advice and believed in my project all along the way. The anonymous readers for Northwestern University Press gave me valuable critiques. I would like to thank the staff members of Northwestern University Press for their work on the different stages of the manuscript. Many other people and organizations have supported me and contributed either directly or indirectly to my ideas for this book: the Association for Pacific Rim Universities, Lorraine Anderson, Bettina Aptheker, Kathy Boardman, Rian Bowie, Gabe Brahm, Julie Brown, Jane Bunker, Rachel Chatham, Valerie Cohen, Toni Crossen, Jim Crosswhite, Roberta Culbertson, Jane Detweiler, Dick Drobnick, Timothy Dunphy, Jean and

Larry Edwards, Tim Edwards, Dean Franco, Jennifer Freyd, Dave Frohn-mayer, Dan Gil, Cheryll Glotfelty, Guy Guinn, Donna Haraway, Luce Irigaray, Julie Kimball, Laurence Kirmayer, Corey Lewis, Ruth Leys, Lawrence Loh, Brad Lucas, Naomi Mandel, Tom Mills, Gianna Mosser, the Oregon Humanities Center, Paul Peppis, Peter Raccuglia, Herman Rapaport, Adrienne Rich, Doug Robinson, Bill Rossi, Kathleen Ruff, Winston Satterlee, Steve Shankman, Jan Laurens Siesling, Jaspal Singh, Tom Slater, Barry Stampfl, Dick Stein, Jim Tarter, Marcia Trojan, Steve Tschudi, Tom Vogler, Polly Wasilewski, Brent Wexler, Patricia Yaeger, and Irene van der Zande.

I extend my deep gratitude to my spouse, Mikhail, who provided me with an abundance of critical insights and productive criticisms on this book. Your patience, humor, and sustenance have helped me every bit of the way in this endeavor and in life.

The following chapters have been revised, some extensively, from previously published essays and are printed here with permission. I would like to acknowledge these publications. A version of chapter 1, "Trauma Theory and Its Discontents: The Potentials of Pluralism," originally appeared in *Mosaic: Journal for the Interdisciplinary Study of Literature* 41, no. 2 (June 2008): 149–66, edited by Dawne McCance. I would like to thank the anonymous readers who provided a great deal of nuanced feedback that helped me work out ideas that ended up in this book. A version of chapter 2, "The Role of Place in Remembering: Lan Cao's *Monkey Bridge*," originally appeared in *Studies in the Humanities* 31, no. 2 (2004): 138–62, edited by Tom Slater. I would especially like to express my thanks to *Studies in the Humanities* for being the first journal to publish my work and to the anonymous readers who gave me excep-tional critiques of my work that every junior scholar craves. A version of chapter 3, "The Traumatized Protagonist and Mythic Landscapes: Leslie Marmon Silko's *Ceremony*," appeared in *ISLE: Interdisciplinary Studies in Literature and Environment* 13, no. 2 (2006): 73–92, edited by Scott Slovic. A version of chapter 4, "Wilderness, Loss, and Cultural Contexts in Edward Abbey's *Black Sun*," appeared in *Foreign Literature Studies* 41, no. 2 (June 2008): 20–40, edited by Zhenazhao Nie.

Introduction

This book examines literary trauma theory from its foundations to its implementations and new possibilities. What began as a concern with the limited potential that trauma theory seemed to offer literary scholarship soon turned into excitement with the discovery of its many formulations and applications. I decided to flesh out a more nuanced and flexible concept of trauma after I found a discursive dependence upon a single psychological theory of trauma in literary criticism. This reliance produced a homogenous interpretation of trauma in literature and narrowed the interplay that occurs between language, experience, memory, and place. I embark here on an analysis that reconsiders the meaning and value of traumatic experience by demonstrating the diversity of its forms in contemporary American novels in an effort to deepen the discussion of trauma beyond that of the disease-driven paradigm in literary criticism today. My critique of the traditional conceptualization of trauma as an inherently unintegrated event that pathologically fragments the self leads me toward the articulation of a new model and approach. This model views trauma and the process of remembering within a framework that emphasizes the multiplicity of responses to an extreme experience and the importance of contextual factors in determining the significance of the event. In order to demonstrate this new approach, I focus my discussion on late-modern canonical and emergent American novels that deal with trauma.

In analyzing the narrative methods authors employ to portray suffering, I found two major patterns: the use of landscape imagery to convey the effects of trauma and remembering, and the use of place as a site that shapes the protagonist's experience and perception of the world. The focus on place in these fictional descriptions brought me to the significance of contextual factors in determining the value of trauma. I discovered that an environmental ethos takes shape in fiction and forms a geographically specific contextual factor of place that influences the representational contingencies of trauma, memory, and the self. What I mean by an environmental ethos is the way in which landscape in the world of the novel creates and defines notions of culture, identity, memory, and place, along with the contradictions of such imaginings. The landscape is shown in the novel as a source, however partial or ambivalent it may be, that expresses epistemological constructs, thus developing the value of experience. The novels under discussion express trauma through a range of values that include negative, positive, neutral, or ambiguous connotations, thereby displacing the dominant claim that attaches only a negative value to trauma. The plethora of different images of trauma in fiction provides diverse views regarding the role of loss and pain in a society and the ways that a society's ethical values are conveyed through the description of suffering.

Trauma commonly refers to an individual's emotional response to an experience that disrupts previously held perceptions of one's self and others. Psychologist Richard McNally suggests three variables that may figure into defining trauma: "an objectively defined event, the person's subjective interpretation of its meaning, and the person's emotional reaction to it. The definitional process is fraught with complexities" (78). Part of the problem of defining trauma arises due to the fact that the European etiology of trauma has been studied without identifying an ultimate cause of symptoms or providing an ultimate solution to symptoms. Nonetheless, profound events are ascribed value by individuals and societies, and the novel as a cultural artistic production puts into play these variations of value. The novel itself offers its own theories, as I delineate in the following chapters, including the view that trauma may cause pathology or may transform consciousness and catalyze a change in perception that allows one to reconstitute identity in a nonpathological fashion. I show that in the novels under discussion, the reorientation of perception is expressed through landscape imagery. Literature elicits numerous representations of trauma, often emphasizing the contextual factors and place-based aspects of an extreme experience. The terms of trauma in literature vary tremendously, especially in fiction, yet there is little debate in literary studies about the concept of trauma or how psychological theories are implemented.

I refer to the currently popular employment of only one psychological model of trauma by literary critics as the traditional model because of its dominance and canonization. Most literary trauma scholars have relied exclusively on the traditional model of trauma, to the extent that a critical trope of fragmentation has emerged as the prevailing rhetoric in trauma studies. This model claims that traumatic experience is not properly registered in memory. As such, the event will never be normally incorporated into consciousness, thus leading to a fragmented sense of self and producing a type of memory with pathological symptoms in which the experience is inaccessibly frozen and unrepresentable. Feelings attached to the experience are only felt through a recollection, never as a direct response to the event, and due to this one must abreact the event in order to ever come close to knowing what happened.

The psychological premise of the traditional model holds that the primary response to trauma is the abnormal division of consciousness. However, the manifold imagery of trauma in literature requires a theoretical pluralism that draws upon various models of trauma and memory that includes dominant and non-dominant psychological concepts in order to account for its diverse representations. Embarking upon a methodology that embraces a theoretical diversity means moving beyond the dominant model to include alternative theories in order to conceptually address the spectrum of traumatic imagery in literature.

In contrast to the traditional model, a more useful methodology is offered by a plurality of psychological theories that concede more than merely a pathological paradigm. In addition to the dominant psychological theories on trauma and memory by Charcot, Freud, Janet, and Breuer, this model employs the theories of other psychiatrists and psychologists such as Laurence Kirmayer, Frederic Bartlett, Craig Piers, and Colin Ross. In a pluralistic model, the concept of trauma is theorized from multiple sources and not restricted to the discourse of the unrepresentable. Rather, trauma is conceptualized to acknowledge pathological responses but not to the exclusion of other responses. Importantly, a pluralistic model describes the multifaceted functions and effects of a traumatic experience in terms that extend past essentialist notions of identity, experience, and remembering found within the traditional model because it conceptualizes memory differently.

As the following chapter will demonstrate, the concept of memory and how it is theorized directly influences the implementation of a literary trauma theory. The pluralistic model entertains a view of remembering as a fluid and selective process of interpretation, rather than only as a literal, veridical recall. Remembering therefore can be influenced by multiple internal and external factors, such as individual personality traits, family history, culture, geographic location, place, and historical period that shape the meaning of an experience. These contextual factors, especially society, cultural values, and landscape are interacting and influencing the process of remembering. This view of memory has many repercussions in terms not only of how one understands the process of remembering, but also how experience is interpreted and accorded value.

In the pluralistic model, the meaning of a traumatic experience can be determined by a remembering process that is open to alteration over time by the individual who continuously revises memories, including those of traumatic experiences, in each moment of remembrance. If remembering a traumatic experience is conceived as an imaginative process of recollection, a process consistently in creation and shaped as much by social narratives as by individual character traits, then in order to understand trauma, attention must be given to the contextual factors that influence both the experience and act of remembering. Considering remembering as an active process of constructions allows for a formulation of trauma beyond that of only a pathologically fixed memory and unrepresentable experience. Because the value and qualities of trauma change over time depending on contextual factors such as cultural values and social narratives, trauma is imagined also as mutable and transitional, rather than only as a dissociated entity that orbits consciousness, or as an inherently wordless event that creates an unknowable memory or mental illness.

Utilizing a pluralistic model for the practice of literary trauma theory allows for a closer examination of the ways that contextual factors such as place and society inform the experience, remembrance, and retelling of a traumatic experience in a novel. In fictional portrayals of trauma, the contextual factors of experience and remembering, particularly place and landscape, are meaning-making sites that portray the wide-ranging signification of emotional suffering. The term "place" refers to a physical environment that is inhabited or imagined by a person who attaches and derives meaning from it. Yi-Fu Tuan suggests that a physical space becomes defined as a place when it is endowed with value: "Place is a special kind of object. It is a concretion of value . . . it is an object in which one can dwell" (12). Place is not only a location of experience, but is also an entity that organizes memories, feelings, and meaning for the individual and for groups.[1] William Lang argues that place is a "dimension of human perception" because "natural forces mix dynamically with social and cultural forces to create distinct and recognizable places" (88). Lawrence Buell suggests that the concept of place "gestures in at least three directions at once—toward environmental materiality, toward social perception or construction, and toward individual affect or bond" (63). In many narrative instances, the description of place in the novel's representations of trauma situates the individual experience within a larger cultural context that shapes the memory and value of an event. Complementing Tuan's definition, D. W. Meinig suggests that place is "some kind of location and ensemble of features. Such things are human creations, in the sense of perceptions, a mental imposition of order, a parcelization of the earth's surface, a transformation of space—an abstraction—into something more specific and limited" (1). The representation of place in narrative descriptions of trauma carries individual and social values that direct the understanding and remembrance of trauma. Place is thus a central aspect of traumatic experience in literary representations because place provides a conceptual framework in which emotional responses occur.

In the novels discussed here, one can imagine place as the silent second character, for it is the geographic location, cultural influence, and historical moment that merge to define the value of trauma for the individual and community. Place often functions as a generative site for meaning in the novel because it influences the emotional texture, cognitive codification, and narrative form of the event, rather than standing solely as a backdrop screen for the action of the plot. At times, a place in nature is the arena where the literal and metaphoric actions of the plot reach a catharsis because the land is the location where the protagonist comes to terms with memories of a traumatic experience. For several novels in this study, landscape imagery functions as a preferred medium to portray the effects of trauma on consciousness and, in particular, the dissociative states of the mind, which is one among many types of responses to trauma.

Certain novels demonstrate through different narrative techniques that an extreme experience can elicit a disruption in perception or a transformation of consciousness that illuminates the dynamics of memory and identity. One strategy employed to convey a type of disruption is narrative dissociation. Dissociation in the narrative, or narrative dissociation, defines the literary representation of an altered state of consciousness that disrupts and reorients a character's perceptions. Psychological dissociation refers to "shifts in mental states or voices" and can be understood as a period when the self experiences two states of consciousness or perspectives (Kirmayer 180). Psychiatrist Laurence Kirmayer notes that dissociation is often referred to as a rigid walling off of experience, but it is actually more fluid: "In clinical reality, as in the laboratory, dissociation is found in all degrees of intensity in the same individual and is characterized by its fluidity" (180). Kirmayer demonstrates that trauma may produce a variety of responses including but not limited to amnesia or repression, rather than dissociation, depending on the type of experience.[2]

Strategies of expressing dissociation include the disjunction of time through the use of repetition and negation; imagistic scenes of violence that lack emotional description; syntactical subversion and rearrangement; atemporality; and a doubled consciousness or point of view. These narrative techniques show the multiple sites of tension that arise within the protagonist and highlight the personal and cultural spheres of action that inform the emotional experience. The lack of cohesion and the disturbance of previous formulations of self and reality are sometimes conveyed in the form of an interruptive or nonlinear narrative. In addition, a temporally disjointed narrative highlights the struggle of the protagonist to identify the meaning and purpose of an experience.

Narrative dissociation is similar to the method of stream of consciousness, but exhibits some differences. Stream of consciousness is defined as "a special mode of narration that undertakes to capture the full spectrum of the *continuous flow* of a character's mental process, in which sense perceptions mingle with conscious and half-conscious thoughts, memories, expectations, feelings, and random associations" (Abrams 180, italics mine). Edward Bloom argues that the stream of consciousness technique is employed to show the *association* of thoughts and to "represent the flux of thoughts and emotions which succeed each other in a random rather than logical manner" (158–60, italics mine). Narrative dissociation could be considered a subgenre of the stream of consciousness strategy in that both techniques attempt to express how the mind works and the relation between internal and external realities. However, narrative dissociation creates several different effects. The mode of narrative dissociation emphasizes the difference rather than sameness of thoughts and perceptions. Instead of a continuous flow or association of thoughts, there is a cacophony of feelings and perceptions that produces a disjunction, which is often portrayed as a doubling. The process of doubling or expressing two states of consciousness can occur when the traumatic past is brought into conflict with the present in order to portray the character's emotional struggle. The mode of doubling can also depict an alternate reality or point of view occurring simultaneously with the current reality in order to portray the character's imaginative effort to remove himself from the present moment of harm. The method of narrative dissociation takes as its subject matter the process of doubling that shows how feelings become dis-associated rather than associated. The modes of narrative dissociation bring us back to the significance accorded to place in fictional descriptions of trauma because place has the ability to explain the emotional experience in terms not only of the physical environment, but also in relation to particular landscapes and communities.

My book begins by providing a theoretical framework to discuss trauma and memory in novels. The first chapter analyzes the trends in literary trauma theory and the consequences of relying upon a single trauma model. I examine the debate on trauma within psychological and literary fields, primarily regarding the influence of traumatic experience on memory and identity. My discussion explores the significance of contextual factors at work in both the experience and remembrance of trauma, indicating that a pluralistic model would allow greater interpretive avenues to explore the nature of trauma in literature.

In the following chapters I move into an analysis of four contemporary American novels and their narrative methods, illustrating how each novel's reliance on place opens new avenues to investigate the topic of trauma for critical theory. The second chapter addresses Lan Cao's novel *Monkey Bridge* (1997), a work that offers the opportunity to study narrative dissociation and the variety of responses to trauma. The novel indicates that trauma, for the female Vietnamese protagonists, is not understood merely as a universal response to the collective event of war. Rather, it is an experience defined by personal peculiarities and social contingencies, such as culture, family ties, national myths, and the relationship to a place, specifically the rural lands in the Mekong Delta. The novel's depictions of trauma remind us that individual memories are related to a place that has social and political values, forms of language, and even ideologies that guide how the story of trauma is interpreted and expressed.

In the third chapter I examine the ways that identity and traumatic memories are connected to both the intimate relationship with a homeland and the social pressures created by the protagonist's community in Leslie Marmon Silko's *Ceremony* (1977). I explore the function of the traumatized protagonist in fiction, which challenges the concept of transhistorical trauma. The pressures to ascribe a certain value to the traumatic past are socially driven and include directives from a tribal-mythic narrative that suggests the protagonist's struggle with his personal past symbolically correlates to the historical struggle of Native Americans to survive colonization. I argue that the land is both the source of trauma and the site of healing for the protagonist.

In the fourth chapter I explore how loss alters identity through a Renaissance humanist paradigm in Edward Abbey's novel *Black Sun* (1971). Traumatic loss forces the protagonist to reframe his subjectivity in relation to an external world that shifts between being a familiar and a foreign entity, thereby unsettling the protagonist's attempts to reformulate his sense of self. The novel demonstrates that traumatic memory is an active and revisionary process, thus upsetting the dominant model that claims trauma remains fixed and separated from "normal" memories.

Chapter 5 turns to Robert Barclay's *Melal* (2002), a novel that develops a relationship between the traumatic atomic past and the neocolonial present through a family living in the Marshall Islands. Poverty and pollution comprise daily existence in the rural atolls in the Pacific, but a resilient self emerges through the creation of new narratives of identity linked to notions of mortality, the afterlife, and the American capitalist market. However, this subjectivity is not tied necessarily to a nation, a national consciousness, or even a postcolonial identity. The conflict that shapes identity in this novel is ecological and social devastation caused by military bombs and nuclear tests, which force the Marshallese protagonists to reposition their sense of self in relation to a largely uninhabitable landscape.

Trauma in the novel is an evocation of suffering that invites the reader to see over the edge of her own life in order to cultivate an understanding of another. Literature provides a unique view of consciousness just as psychology offers its own. But perhaps it is not such a different view, just a different methodology, since both fields are in the business of interpretation. Sigmund Freud might agree, reminding us in "Beyond the Pleasure Principle" that "psychoanalysis was above all an art of interpretation" (22). The novel offers an artistic interpretation of consciousness that draws attention to areas of human experience that might be overlooked or denied in society and brings the discussion of trauma into public view. Taking up this conversation in the following pages, I explore the ways that narrative depictions express and ascribe value to trauma and the process of remembering.

THE NATURE OF TRAUMA
IN AMERICAN NOVELS

Trauma Theory and Its Discontents
The Potentials of Pluralism

The growing interest in the topic of trauma within literary criticism began in the 1990s. Yet, since Kali Tal's *Worlds of Hurt: Reading the Literatures of Trauma* (1996) and Cathy Caruth's *Unclaimed Experience* (1996), most analyses regularly employ a narrow definition of trauma culled from only one among many psychological theories, despite the fact that psychology research has produced a multifaceted and at times contentious body of work on the subject over the centuries.[1] Literary trauma theory is a burgeoning discipline that examines extreme emotional states and profound changes of perception in a text by utilizing psychological theories on trauma and memory.

However, the popular reliance on a single model of trauma in criticism over the last two decades has created a limited method of interpretation that fails to adequately address the complex phenomena of trauma in literature. To date, the methodology of literary trauma scholars has been largely influenced by a selective use of psychology theories that builds a solitary paradigm of pathology to explain trauma. This method of analysis has produced the traditional model that claims trauma is a speechless void, unrepresentable, inherently pathologic, timeless, and repetitious. A major assumption of this model that allows these claims to be made relies upon a monocular view of memory. Employing new theoretical perspectives and methodologies avoids developing an essentialist trauma discourse in a significant and still emerging field of study.

Appreciating what is at stake in the differing theories of trauma begins with a brief return to early researchers. Significant aspects of our late-modern concept of trauma originate in the world of nineteenth-century research. Psychological models of trauma and memory can be found in the work of John Eric Erichsen, Sir James Paget, J. M. Charcot, and Hermann Oppenheim. Sources that most literary critics cite include work by Sigmund Freud, Josef Breuer, Morton Prince, Abram Kardiner, and Pierre Janet, who all published extensively on trauma.[2] Charcot, the French neurobiologist, published research on what he called traumatic hysteria, which he defined as physical symptomatology arising from intense fright. The German neurologist Oppenheim disagreed with Charcot's conception of trauma and his pairing of hysterias with trauma cases. Oppenheim defined "traumatic neurosis" as a condition that originated from somatic and psychogenic sources (Micale and Lerner 15). Later, the neurologist Sigmund Freud developed a theory of psychological trauma that has become a major source for the practice of traditional literary trauma theory.

In *Beyond the Pleasure Principle*, Freud conceives of the mind as an organism that is shielded by a "protective barrier," which is composed of the "central psychic apparatus" that protects the mind from "harmful stimuli" (31, 34). Freud writes: "I think one may venture (tentatively) to regard ordinary traumatic neurosis as the result of an extensive rupture of the barrier against stimuli" (36). His theory declares that trauma "breaks through" into the mind that is unprepared for such stimulation, causing unexpected emotional shock (19). This sudden shock causes the individual to repeat the event in order to gain mastery over feelings of shock, fright, and apprehension (36–37). Freud suggests several possibilities for the mental mechanisms that cause traumatic responses and the forms of treatment to reduce debilitating symptoms. He explains that the patient must abreact the traumatic experience in hypnosis or talk to a therapist in order to achieve a cathartic recovery. However, Freud questions if all external events in the life of an individual leave permanent traces in the mind, which form the foundations of memory-records that can be retrieved through the talking cure and "working through" (Breuer 272; Freud [1914] 1955:150). Even though Freud remains uncertain in his writings about the effects of trauma on memory and questions the possibility that traumatic neurosis can be reversed through the "talking cure," his initial theories that trauma is a result of a rupture or break are cited by literary critics as the foundational basis for the traditional model.

Pierre Janet also wrote extensively on traumatic responses, but was equally ambiguous regarding trauma's origins and effects (672–74). Even with the contradictions and uncertainties in their research, both Freud and Janet are significant to our understanding of trauma, especially for their views that trauma "infects" the individual. For Janet, his focus remained on the lasting effects of a traumatic event within the individual. Janet argues that traumatic symptoms are governed by "subconscious fixed ideas" (13). He argues that traumatic events produce a traumatic memory, which is different than ordinary memory: "Strictly speaking, then, one who retains a fixed idea of a happening cannot be said to have a 'memory' of the happening. It is only for convenience that we speak of it as a 'traumatic memory'. The subject is often incapable of making with regard to the event the recital which we speak of as a memory . . ." (663). Janet claims that trauma is stored differently in the brain and separated from quotidian experiences where it remains fixed and returns repeatedly to "haunt" the individual (661). He imagines memory as a "storehouse" where all experiences are stored in the mind and can be retrieved exactly as they occurred. Janet emphasizes the need to remember the past and narrativize the traumatic experience in order to integrate the event into what he calls "normal memory." However, Janet remains inconsistent in his writings on trauma and memory; at certain moments he insists on the importance of remembering and verbalizing the past trauma, while at other times he encourages the patient to forget (421).

A compelling overview regarding the historical antecedents to the traditional model of trauma in our contemporary moment is found in Ruth Leys's study *Trauma: A Genealogy* (2000). Leys documents the historical developments regarding the concept of trauma, a concept that she argues has alternated between a mimetic and an antimimetic model. The mimetic model suggests that trauma can only be understand as involving an "imitation or identification in which, precisely because the victim cannot recall the original traumatogenic event, she is fated to act it out or in other ways imitate it" (298). The antimimetic model suggests that "the idea of trauma is a purely external event that befalls a fully constituted subject" (299). Leys examines the psychological and theoretical limitations of the traditional mimetic/antimimetic models that produce a highly unstable concept of trauma.

The popular notion in literary criticism that trauma inherently produces a temporal gap and a pathologically fragmented self works from a Freudian perspective of the mind that imagines normal external stimuli enter the brain in one fashion, but traumatic stimuli enter another region of the brain in a different fashion. Starting from this theoretical vantage point, literary trauma scholars have created a trend of defining traumatic experience as a timeless void that "shatters" identity, producing a long-lasting muteness and lack of knowledge regarding the exact event. Because a traumatic event is never properly experienced or registered as a memory, it is never normally incorporated into consciousness. This leads to a fractured pathological self and memory. Such a model produces the notion that trauma is a prelinguistic event—it invades the mind with such unexpected ferocity that language fails to code it. Due to this unspeakable experience, the only response to representation is achieved through abreaction. Demonstrating this view, literary scholar Kali Tal argues, "Accurate representation of trauma can never be achieved without recreating the event since, by its very definition, trauma lies beyond the bounds of 'normal' conception" (15). This concept of trauma and memory emphasizes the necessity to re-create or abreact through narrative recall. Yet, at the same time, the remembrance of trauma is always an approximate account of the past, since traumatic experience precludes knowledge and hence representation. The model implemented here considers the responses to trauma, including cognitive chaos and the possible division of consciousness, as inherent characteristics of traumatic experience and memory. In this model, a traumatic experience disturbs consciousness to such a degree that identity and memory remain confused and divided, and only in the attempt to abreact the event through the act of narration may the individual come close to experiencing it.

The traditional model is perhaps best demonstrated by literary critic Cathy Caruth in her book *Unclaimed Experience: Trauma, Narrative, and History*. The prevalent view in literary trauma studies today that "trauma stands outside representation altogether" imagines an intrinsic epistemological fissure between traumatic experience and representation (17). Caruth argues that "trauma is not locatable in the simple violent or original event in an individual's past, but rather in the way its very unassimilated nature—the way it was precisely *not known* in the first instance—returns to haunt the survivor later on" (4). Traumatic experience is unrepresentable due to the inability of the brain, understood as the carrier of coherent cognitive schematas, to properly encode and process the event. The origin of traumatic response is forever unknown and unintegrated; yet the ambiguous, literal event is ever-present and intrusive. Caruth also explains trauma as "a shock that appears to work very much like a bodily threat but is in fact a break in the mind's experience of time" (61). Trauma is imagined here as something that disrupts without pain and creates a temporal gap. Caruth says that trauma is only known through repetitive flashbacks that literally reenact the event because the mind cannot represent it otherwise: "The historical power of trauma is not just that the experience is repeated after its forgetting, but that it is only in and through its inherent forgetting that it is first experienced at all" (17).

The model exemplified by Caruth defines trauma in terms of the abnormal division of consciousness that leads to the unrepresentable nature of trauma, and perceives all responses to an extreme experience as fundamentally pathologic and divisive. This view is upheld by the idea that a causal connection exists between trauma and dissociation, that is, that trauma directly induces dissociation. The position does not allow for the distinction between the experience of disruption that may or may not produce a temporal gap and the experience of dissolution that erases knowledge. In addition, the view that all responses to any kind of extreme experience produce fragmentation and epistemological erasure perpetuates the idea of the inherent pathology of traumatic experience and responses. In *Unclaimed Experience*, Caruth relies upon the psychological research of experts such as Judith Herman and Bessel van der Kolk who emphasize the causal relation between trauma and dissociation, which informs the foundations of her literary trauma theory. Importantly, this model of trauma emphasizes the need to re-create through narration the traumatic event in order to attempt to assimilate trauma into the "normal memory," as defined by Janet.

Judith Herman's *Trauma and Recovery* (1992) is an important analysis in many ways due to its examination of the evolution of the psychological definition of trauma and the stages of recovery. Although Herman does address social dimensions of trauma, she relies upon neurobiological models to assert that there exists a direct causal link between trauma and dissociation, a claim strongly disputed by psychiatrists and psychologists. Herman argues:

> Traumatic exposure can produce lasting alterations in
> the endocrine, autonomic, and central nervous systems. . . .
> Dissociation appears to be the mechanism by which in-
> tense sensory and emotional experiences are disconnected
> from the social domain of language and memory, the
> internal mechanism by which terrorized people are
> silenced. (238–39)

Herman takes a neuro-hormonal premise to examine memory functions and trauma's effects on the individual to suggest that a female rape victim's response to trauma is similar if not the same to that of the male combat veteran. This move to connect the experience of trauma across genders based upon biological brain functions seems to serve a larger agenda of the book to raise public awareness about female rape and domestic violence against women in the United States.

Herman's theoretical orientation regarding the processes of remembering, memory's influence on consciousness, and the individual's concept of self before and after the event determine how much significance is ascribed to the narrative recall or abreaction of trauma in order to recover. Herman claims trauma's effect on the individual can be reversed through talking to another person. She cites T. Kean's experiments to argue: "It appears, then, that the 'action of telling a story' in the safety of a protected relationship can actually produce a change in the abnormal processing of the traumatic memory. . . . The *physioneurosis* induced by terror can apparently be reversed through the use of words" (183). To recover, according to this view, one must place the traumatic experience into a narrative to be told to another because the memory of the traumatic event is understood as a literal and fixed record of experience stored in an area of the brain that can be unlocked by talking. Abreaction and narrative recall are regarded as the key to unlock the door to the frozen memory. Importantly, Herman argues that traumatic events "shatter the construction of the self that is formed and sustained in relation to others" (51). The discourse of shattering might be traced back to Ronnie Janoff-Bulman's widely circulated and cited article published in 1985 which introduced the idea of the "shattered assumption" framework for conceptualizing trauma's impact.[3] The idea that trauma "shatters" identity that Herman articulates builds upon Freud's view that trauma "breaks through" the protective barriers of the mind and becomes imprinted without the proper schemata to accommodate it.

Upholding this perspective, psychiatrist Bessel van der Kolk also forwards a neural-hormonal concept of trauma as prelinguistic and thus unspeakable. Van der Kolk writes: "When people are exposed to trauma, that is, a frightening event outside of ordinary human experience, they experience 'speechless terror.' The experience cannot be organized on a linguistic level" (1987: 172). Traumatic experience is "stored differently" causing traumatic memory to become "dissociated from conscious awareness and voluntary control" (160). This yields the unspeakable quality of trauma. Speech is again identified as both the solution to the problem of traumatic pathology and a main feature that, when it is lacking, defines trauma. Van der Kolk's characterization tends to universalize the diverse responses to and consequences of traumatic experience, suggesting that terrifying events affect all people in the same fashion due to its neurobiological basis. The concept of trauma expressed here implies a sense of contagion attached to trauma with the phrase "exposed to trauma," suggesting trauma acts like a disease or virus. In addition, the fragmentation model of trauma implies that the self is a fixed entity, already constructed and unchanging before the event. This contrasts with other models that allow a view of the self as a relational entity, one that is in flux and contingent upon an assortment of contextual factors. Moreover, van der Kolk's and Herman's views that universal neural-hormonal changes occur in response to a traumatic experience and the claim that trauma and dissociation are causal continue to be contested by psychiatrists (Young 277, 284).[4] Allan Young argues for the variance of trauma found in psychological research:

> From the nineteenth century on, it has been observed that
> people do not respond uniformly when exposed to the same
> potentially traumatizing event. . . . Encounters with death
> and injury affect different people in different ways, *also* . . .
> different people can have profoundly different conceptions
> of what constitutes a realistic "threat." (284–89)

That people react differently to traumatic events, even in terms of neu-robiological responses, is a view that challenges the theoretical foundation of the traditional model. In terms of responses to trauma, the difficulty of speaking about a traumatic experience is not necessarily due to the intrinsic quality of trauma to defy all representation, but due to variable factors, including individual, social, and cultural factors that influence the remembrance and narration of the experience. The "speechless terror" or unspeakable quality of trauma as a fixed response should not be taken as an irrefutable fact or as the inherent quality of traumatic experience. Especially because psychological research questions this claim, it is imperative that literary trauma theory, which is dependent upon a psychological theory, treads carefully with the application of dissociation in relation to trauma. In other words, it should not be taken for granted that the universal response to trauma is dissociation or that trauma is causally connected to dissociation. Dissociation is represented in fiction, often associated with trauma, but fictional representations do not necessarily indicate that dissociation is the only response to trauma, nor do novels only show that traumatic memories are stored separately in different areas of the brain. A pathological response or symptom is one response of many identified in psychology studies as well as in literature, but it must not be taken as an irrefutable scientific truth that trauma is directly linked to dissociation when the scientific community itself is in disagreement over what trauma is and how or why dissociation occurs.

The view that trauma pathologically fragments consciousness assumes a causal link between trauma and dissociation, yet this causality maintains skepticism within the psychology field. While psychological research shows that trauma connotes disruption and discontinuity in the perception of self and reality, there remains disagreement in the psychology field over what defines trauma and the claim that traumatic events directly cause dissociation or a "structural breakdown" in identity (Becker 106). Richard McNally points out the problem of defining trauma when he writes that trauma "might be defined by the objective attributes of the stressor, by the subjective response of the victim, or by both" (79). The *Diagnostic and Statistical Manual of Mental Disorders* states that traumatic stressors are "actual or threatened death or serious injury, or a threat to the physical integrity of self and others [that produce] intense fear, helplessness, or horror" (American Psychiatric Association 427–28). Surviving war, sexual abuse, slavery, or natural disasters are extreme threats that can be followed by what psychologist David Becker calls a "chaotic response" of the mind (Becker 105). Research by psychiatrist Laurence Kirmayer shows that victims of torture, violence, and abuse "report a degree of alienation and estrangement from self and others that throws into high relief the tacit dimensions of social life" (182). The *Comprehensive Textbook of Psychiatry* states that psychological trauma is characterized by feelings of "intense fear, helplessness, loss of control, and threat of annihilation" (Sadock, Sadock, and Ruiz 918). These feelings can create major disruptions in the individual's perception of self and reality, assumption of safety in the world, and the connections to family and community members. Extreme experiences may produce feelings of fear, anxiety, betrayal, and shock, which under certain circumstances and factors may lead to dissociation or psychic splitting, but pathological dissociation is not the direct causal result or only result.[5] Kirmayer explains: "The direct linkage of trauma and dissociation appears simplistic in the face of research demonstrating the effects of temperament, family history, psychopathology, and current context on dissociation" (180). This highlights a commonly acknowledged position in psychology that is ignored in literary studies. Furthermore, this position on trauma and dissociation undermines a major functioning assumption of the traditional model: there is no consensus today among psychiatrists and psychologists regarding a causal link between a traumatic experience and dissociation. The perspective that dissociation is not an inherent response to an extreme event should allow the literary scholar to avoid using dissociation as a shorthand for traumatic experience.

However, the traditional model of trauma employs as one of its theoretical foundations a direct causal link between trauma and dissociation, claiming that trauma pathologically divides the self and destroys knowledge. This model claims that traumatic experience is timeless and unknowable, yet it is also a literal, repetitious event that is imagined as a disease that can be transmitted to others. Trauma has the potential to *infect* another. Demonstrating this model again is Caruth in *Unclaimed Experience:* "The experience of a trauma repeats itself, exactly and unremittingly, through the unknowing acts of the survivor and against his very will" (2). This model imagines external events happening to a passive subject, upon which infectious pathogens wiggle into the mind, take a seat, and cause harm. Yet, the contradiction of the traditional model is that while the experience is isolated in the brain, it still carries the potential to infect another pure and integrated subject through the act of narration, or based upon common ancestry or ethnic origins. Caruth suggests that traumatic experience is contagious by stating that trauma "is never simply one's own . . . [but] precisely the way we are implicated in each other's traumas" (24). The contagion theory of an unidentifiable, yet infectious, pathogen allows Caruth to claim that traumatic experience is transhistorically passed across generations, primarily through verbal or written acts of remembering. This standpoint helps to support claims that suggest since traumatic experience is intergenerationally transmitted based on shared characteristics, then everyone can experience trauma through vicarious means based on a shared ethnic, racial, national, or economic background, thereby producing what Kirby Farrell calls a "posttraumatic culture" (3).[6]

The traditional formulations of trauma and memory exemplified by Caruth have become an important source for the theorization of trauma in literary studies, especially as a source to support the notion of intergenerational or transhistorical trauma. The concept of trauma as timeless, repetitious, and infectious supports a literary theory of transhistorical trauma by making a binary relationship between the individual and group, as well as between traumatic experience and pathological dissociation. The transhistorical trauma theory indicates that a massive trauma experienced by a group in the historical past can be experienced by an individual living centuries later who shares a similar attribute of the historical group, such as sharing the same race, religion, nationality, or gender due to everlasting and universal characteristics of traumatic experience and memory. Conversely, individual trauma can be passed to others of a shared ethnic, racial, or gender group who did not experience the actual event, but because they share social or biological similarities, the traumatic experience of the individual and group becomes one. This supports the claim that narratives can re-create and abreact the traumatic experience for those who were not there—the reader, listener, or witness can experience the historical trauma firsthand.[7] Therefore, historical traumatic experience is the source that marks and defines contemporary individual identity, as well as racial or cultural identity.

However, the theory of transhistorical trauma limits the meaning of trauma in literature because it conflates the distinctions between personal loss actually experienced by an individual and a historical absence found in one's ancestral lineage. Personal loss can be understood as the lived experience of a traumatic event by an individual. Historical absence is a historically documented loss that was experienced by a person's ancestors. Dominick LaCapra elucidates the distinction between loss and absence when he says that people face "particular losses in distinct ways," as opposed to a historical absence of experience that was never there to begin with and therefore cannot be experienced as a lack or loss (1999:700). The theory of intergenerational trauma combines loss and absence and collapses the boundaries between the individual and group, thereby suggesting that a person's identity can be vicariously traumatized by reading a historical narrative or due to a shared genealogy that affords the label of victim as part of personal or public identity. In addition, blurring the distinction between absence and loss could lead to the view that both victim and perpetrator maintain the same relationship to a traumatic experience and exhibit the same responses.

The conceptualization of the connection between trauma experienced by an individual versus that experienced by a group works within a larger debate regarding identity formation, especially racial identity formation. This theory establishes an essentialist concept of identity organized around a notion of the intergenerational sharing of loss and suffering because the actual event is transmitted to descendants of a common racial, ethnic, national, religious, class, or gender group. An example of an experience that could be viewed as producing a historical absence is the socioeconomic institution of slavery in North America, which denied human rights to African slaves and their descendants for decades. Slavery produced a historical absence for the descendants of slaves whose ancestors were not granted citizenship and all ensuing rights and protections. There is little doubt that the historical lack of rights for black Americans has created socioeconomic inequalities for black Americans today. However, the historical absence of citizenship and civic rights is employed by some to claim that descendants of the same group, based on shared ethnicity or genealogy, experience psychological trauma from this historical event in the present day.

A representative example of transhistorical trauma theory that informs an argument about racial identity formation in literature is found in J. Brooks Bouson's *Quiet as It's Kept: Shame, Trauma, and Race in the Novels of Toni Morrison* (2000). The book argues that the traumatic experience of slavery and "white racist practices" throughout history have produced a "learned cultural shame" that is an inherent quality of contemporary black identity and of the "collective African-American experience" which appears in Morrison's fiction and American culture at large (4). Bouson offers useful insights on Morrison's writing practices, but maintains an essentialist rhetoric regarding trauma and (racial) identity in an effort to link the current violence and despair of a racial group in America today to the violence and oppression experienced by the same historical racial and/or cultural group centuries earlier through a reliance on transhistorical trauma theory.[8]

The idea of the infectious potential of a response to a traumatic experience supports Bouson's position that a historical experience of violence defines (racial) identity. First, a traditionalist notion of trauma is introduced which accepts that all responses to trauma are universally pathological and divisive, thereby upholding a causal relationship between traumatic experience and dissociation: "Morrison represents the speechless terror of trauma in recurring scenes of dissociated violence" (3). The definition of trauma here is based on an abreactive model in which the "speechless terror" of trauma (a term from Bessel van der

Kolk's *Psychological Trauma*) refers to the temporal-linguistic gap induced by the experience. Then, the notion of universal responses to trauma is established by such claims as: "dissociation, rather than repression, is *common* to the trauma experience," and that "traumatic experiences become encoded in an abnormal type of memory" (7, emphasis added). Although dissociation can indeed occur in relation to violence or oppression, there are ample examples in psychology studies and literary representations that dissociation and speechlessness are not the only response to events. Different types of traumas produce different responses, such as dissociative amnesia or intrusive recall, which are a result of many factors (Kirmayer 184). As discussed earlier, some traumatic experiences can produce dissociation, while this is not the only response. Dissociation is an alteration of consciousness that may or may not carry negative results or pathological symptoms. Psychologists Lisa Butler and Oxana Palesh explain different forms of dissociation and examine the dissociation that occurs when people watch movies.[9]

Bouson establishes a notion of trauma as a contagious and universally experienced phenomenon to argue that the "collective memories" of slavery are "intergenerationally transmitted" specifically and only to African Americans (3, 5). She argues that all black Americans in the United States are fundamentally traumatized victims due to slavery in previous decades because these collective memories of slavery "haunt" descendants of slaves. These memories reinscribe the trauma and shame that are assumed to have been experienced by an individual's ancestors. Here, the transhistorical capacity of trauma employs an essentialist concept of identity which is tied to a traditional model of trauma that declares there is a universally shared (neural-hormonal) response to traumatic experience, thus indicating that individual identity is defined by a certain historical experience of her racial, religious, or gender group.

This perspective depends upon a conflation of traumatic loss and historical absence in order to articulate a fixed identity that is created by transhistorical trauma. It produces a contradictory position because the theory appears to suggest that historical trauma is the basis of identity, which allows for certain peoples who did not experience trauma to appropriate particular traumas by other groups in a movement of identity formation that relies upon traumatic events for value in society. The assumed causal link between collective and individual experience obscures the different forms of violence, torture, and abuse that can produce different responses in different individuals. Importantly, this model of trauma and memory asserts, on the one hand, that trauma is hermeneutically sealed or dissociated. On the other hand, it can be passed between generations, which therefore undoes its own referential basis because once trauma is "spoken" and passed to another, it no longer remains unspeakable, and thus no longer "traumatic" according to the model's own definition of the term.

When Bouson suggests that the historical oppression of a group categorized under the term African American produces a special "traumatized" social status, I see a desire to point to the injustice and pain of this group or others related to the group. But this perspective elides the contemporary processes that produce and enact ideologies of racial superiority. This essentialized notion of race insists upon ideologies of racial purity and fixed categories of race, pointing toward a deeper crisis in the conceptualizations of race and identity in society. Samira Kawash argues that race "must be addressed doubly, as both the origin of an absolutely real division and as the project of an utterly false and impossible distinction" (20). The layered dimensions of race are not adequately addressed in the traditional transhistorical trauma model because it restricts definitional concepts of emotional pain, identity, and race, which eventually polarizes the ways that suffering is represented.[10]

The transhistorical theory of trauma and memory offers a rhetorically appealing paradigm with which to examine the function of trauma in literature and its social implications. However, it tends to produce a reductive view of the variety of responses to trauma and the processes of memory and identity formation found in literary representations. The transhistorical model posits an assumed causality between the individual and group, and between experience and pathology, which overlooks an important function of trauma in fiction. The causal error might even be attributed to the formal qualities of fiction itself because trauma in fiction is conveyed through a protagonist that functions as a representative cultural figure. The trick of trauma in fiction is that the individual protagonist functions to express a unique personal traumatic experience, yet the protagonist may also function to represent an event that was experienced by a group of people, either historically based or futuristically imagined. Perhaps for this reason, some critics are quick to employ the transhistorical trauma theory as a means to explain the intersections between personal and social experience.

The traumatized protagonist in fiction brings into awareness the specificity of individual trauma that is often connected to larger social factors and cultural ideologies. Trauma in fiction provides a picture of the individual who suffers, but paints it in such a way as to suggest that this protagonist is an "everyperson" figure. Indeed, a significant purpose of the protagonist is often to reference a historical period in which a group of people or a particular culture, race, or gender have collectively experienced trauma. In this regard, the fictional figure magnifies a historical event in which thousands or millions of people have suffered a similar violence, such as slavery, war, torture, rape, natural disaster, or nuclear devastation. For example, in Leslie Marmon Silko's novel *Ceremony* and Lan Cao's *Monkey Bridge,* the protagonist functions as a cultural figure to raise awareness about a historical event, such as the government seizures of tribal lands and forced assimilation practices endured by Native Americans in Silko's novel, or the civil war in Vietnam and America's increasing military interventions in Cao's novel. However, this imaginative return to or evocation of the historical past in the novel does not indicate that every person associated with that historical group has experienced trauma, or that the historical event is the sole defining feature of a group or individual. The experience of suffering, no matter how private the experience, is situated in relation to the context of a culture that ascribes different value to the experience and to the individual's feelings about the experience. If the self is conceived as a product of both culture and individual idiosyncratic tendencies and behaviors, then it follows that the meaning of trauma is found between the poles of the individual and society. A central thematic dynamic in novels that describe suffering is thus located in the representation of the individual experience of trauma that necessarily oscillates between private and public meanings, between personal and social paradigms.

The protagonists in the novels noted above are shown to experience and remember trauma within the context of a culture that ascribes different layers of meaning to the event. Therefore, the traumatized protagonist carries out a significant component of trauma in fiction by demonstrating the ways that the experience and remembrance of trauma are situated in relation to a specific culture and place. If trauma is represented in relation to the intersection of individual and cultural spheres of action in a novel, then the experiences of the protagonist often reflect larger cultural forces. For example, the mother in Lan Cao's *Monkey Bridge* experiences trauma as a specific event of being wounded as a civilian in a wartime battle, as well as a result of larger karmic cycles in the universe that she believes have doomed her to suffer. Similarly, the protagonist in *Ceremony* views his trauma as resulting from both a specific war experience and a Laguna-mythic battle between good and evil. In this respect, the protagonist conveys manifold meanings that function on individual, cultural, and ideological levels. Taking into account these varied functions and meanings of the protagonist would allow for other analyses of the trauma in literature that include, but move beyond, a pathological paradigm.

To claim that the traumatized protagonist expresses a specific, idiosyncratic response to trauma, while also functioning as representative figure of a social group in order to relate the actions in the novel to a historical event, does not suggest that the protagonist asserts an intergenerational trauma based on a decades-old event. Novels demonstrate the ways that an experience disrupts the individual conceptualizations of self and connections to family and community, but the values attributed to the traumatic experience are also shaped by cultural forces created within the world of the novel.

Although psychiatrists and psychologists disagree over the effects of an extreme experience on the survivor's memory and identity, there is general agreement that traumatic experience can disrupt or alter consciousness, memory, sense of self, and relation to community (Williams and Banyard xi). Yet, to what degree traumatic experience disrupts memory, self, and relation to others is mediated by cultural values and narrative forms rooted in a place that allow or disallow certain emotions to be expressed. Psychiatrist Laurence Kirmayer explains the ways society influences the comprehension of trauma:

> Registration, rehearsal, and recall [of traumatic events] are
> governed by social contexts and cultural models for memories,
> narratives, and life stories. Such cultural models influence
> what is viewed as salient, how it is interpreted and encoded
> at the time of registration, and, most important for long-term
> memories that serve autobiographical functions, what is so-
> cially possible to speak of and what must remain hidden and
> unacknowledged. (191)

Thus, the "speakability" of traumatic experience is influenced by cultural models in the novel which identify the most important aspects
to remember. This perspective reminds us that the "unspeakability" of
trauma claimed by so many literary critics today can be understood less
as an epistemological conundrum or neurobiological fact, but more as
an outcome of cultural values and ideologies.

Considering the multiple functions of the traumatized protagonist in
this light allows for an alternative analysis to that of Bouson's argument
regarding the representations of trauma in Toni Morrison's novels. For
example, in Morrison's novel *Beloved* (1987), Morrison's portrayal of
African American life in post-1865 Ohio is expressed by a traumatized
protagonist, Sethe, who highlights the damaging social institution of
American slavery and the emotional suffering of Africans and black
Americans. To a certain extent, Morrison's construction of a female African American woman's oppression and survival as a slave and a free
person relies upon narrative conventions of nineteenth-century American slave narratives that portray the agony of slavery for African and
black American women. The cruelty and pain endured by female characters in *Beloved* references and modifies the slave narrative themes of
violence, enslavement, and resistance, which are elucidated in, among
other texts, Harriet Jacobs's memoir *Incidents in the Life of a Slave Girl*
(1861). Her memoir provides cultural models and social templates regarding the construction of black female identity that address the oppression and sexual violence experienced by enslaved women.

Harriet Jacobs (pen name Linda Brent) writes about being abused
and raped by her slave master, similar to the experience of the traumatized protagonist in Morrison's novel. Jacobs explains in her narrative

that she tries to tell her grandmother about these experiences of viola-
tion: "My lips moved to make confession, but the words stuck in my
throat. I sat down in the shade of a tree at her door and began to sew"
(387). Later, she writes: "He came every day; and I was subjected to such
insults as no pen can describe. I would not describe them if I could;
they were too low, too revolting" (405). When Jacobs writes that she
cannot describe the physical and sexual abuse because they were "too
revolting," she is employing directives of nineteenth-century social values that stress what is important to convey or what should be withheld
by using a rhetorical technique that implements silence and ambiguity, rather than corporeal description. A critical interpretation that steps
outside the traditional model of trauma suggests that Jacobs makes a
choice to tell or not to tell the reader about the experience with graphic
details. What is withheld from the reader regarding the traumatic experience is conditioned by social standards and narrative conventions
available to a writer at the time of composition that encourage the use of
specific narrative strategies such as narrative omission or lack of vivid
description of the exact experience. Jacobs's use of silence is a strategy
to maintain agency, authorship, and control over the experience by saying in certain regards, "Trust me, you don't want to hear the awful truth
of the experience, but I will let you imagine it yourself." By withholding
an explicit account, the writer creates greater suspense and repulsion
because it allows the reader to imagine his own worst fears of viola-
tion.[11] The omission of detail in Brent's narrative and the emphasis on
silence provide an alternate model of trauma that reflects the rhetoric of
a nineteenth-century social movement that wanted to draw attention to
the effects of slavery in order to abolish the institution and its ideology
of racial superiority.

The rhetorical use of silence in *Incidents in the Life of a Slave Girl* underscores the dehumanizing and torturous effects of slavery on the human body and psyche, yet emphasizes the inner strength and resiliency
of African and black American slaves in North America, which is a perspective articulated more than a century later in Toni Morrison's novel
Beloved. The traumatized protagonist in Morrison's novel is shown as a
figure who becomes emotionally debilitated and even psychotic at one
point, but eventually recovers with the help of her community. Morrison

draws upon a historical figure, Margaret Garner, to guide her construction of the story and the creation of the protagonist Sethe. Similar to the historical person of Garner, Morrison's Sethe escapes a slave plantation, but later threatens to kill her four children when the slave owner finds her. She kills only her infant in order to prevent future enslavement by the white slave master and plantation owner.

The personal experience of slavery, torture, rape, and escape by Morrison's protagonist calls up the experience of a large population from Africa, with a focus on women, who were forcibly transported and enslaved. The protagonist therefore functions to draw a connection between a collective and a personal experience, yet the theoretical leap to claim that this relationship produces a traumatized collective black American identity today depends upon an intergenerational model of trauma and memory. In addition, the character of Beloved is a traumatized protagonist because she symbolically represents the collective experience of Africans enduring the "Middle Passage" journey across the Atlantic from Africa to the Americas (see pages 210–13 in *Beloved*). Viewing Beloved as a metaphoric cultural referent within an alternative trauma model that underscores the function of the traumatized protagonist in fiction therefore destabilizes the attempt to assert the performance of transhistorical trauma in the novel.

Bouson's argument that contemporary racial identity is defined by the "woundedness of African-American life" is better understood when contextualized within the long history of debate in North America by black American scholars, scientists, and artists over how to represent African American life—as a traumatized culture that is a site of radical dislocation and pathology, or as a well-functioning culture with adaptive capacities that is fundamentally healthy (Bouson 21; Berger 58). Therefore, in addition to Bouson's interpretation, Morrison's protagonist can be viewed as exemplifying the notion of the inherent strength of a complex human psyche that prevails against traumatic experiences and moves beyond an identity simply defined by a past traumatic event. The concluding refrain of Morrison's novel, "This is not a story to pass on," invites a variety of interpretations on the ways that personal and collective traumatic experiences are remembered by individuals and by society (275). Rather than suggesting that traumatic experience is a universalized neural-hormonal phenomenon with a genetic imprint in memory, an alternate interpretation suggests that the meaning and value of the story of trauma changes depending on the historical time and place, and that significant lessons can be learned about such a story. The ambiguous refrain of the novel's ending confirms the view that multiple meanings of trauma and memory persist in literary representations. The reference to the multiple functions of silence in the double meaning of the quote above draws attention to the role of silence in expressing trauma in the novel.

Trauma in late-modern American novels conveys a diversity of extreme emotional states through an assortment of narrative innovations, such as landscape imagery, temporal fissures, silence, or narrative omission including the withholding of graphic, visceral details. The text may exhibit a nonlinear plot or disruptive temporal sequences to emphasize mental confusion, chaos, or contemplation as a response to the experience. The strategy of narrative omission that produces a silence may create a "gap" in time, allowing the reader to imagine what might or could have happened to the protagonist, thereby complicating the value and effects of the experience. In terms of Morrison's novel, Naomi Mandel points out that silence and forgetting in *Beloved* "are as much a strategic and self-conscious gesture on the part of the subjugated as they are the product of the subjugating culture's demands and requirements" (172). Although these silences have been seen by literary theorists as proof of trauma's unspeakability, narrative omissions must also be viewed as rhetorical techniques that convey the assorted meanings of trauma. At times, these strategies help the author structure the narrative into a form that attempts to embody the psychological "action" of traumatic memory or dissociation.

Considering the variety of models of memory and dissociation found in a novel leads to a position that reconsiders the common claims about trauma. The novel's expression of painful, incoherent, and transcendent emotional states demonstrates the ways traumatic experience restructures perceptions, as well as the ways that meaning and value are constructed during and after the event. In addition, novels demonstrate that the disruption of previous perceptions of the self or reality does not necessarily confirm the pathological aspects of trauma. In fact, this disruption can work to encourage different forms of knowledge, a process integral to the evolving constitution of identity. In certain novels, silence is created through temporal and spatial disruption to portray the disjointed perception or disparate states of consciousness. In this way, silence is a narrative strategy, rather than evidence for an epistemological void created by the experience of trauma.

The notion that trauma shatters identity and pathologically divides consciousness has become a popular trope for the scholar to define trauma, but in doing so the scholar ascribes universal characteristics to a matrix of intricate emotional responses and combines without distinction the phenomena of traumatic experience and dissociation. Perhaps the traditional concept of trauma is appealing to the scholar because it creates a position to draw attention to the severe pain, both emotional and somatic, caused by external phenomena. The endeavor to acknowledge the experience of pain, however, should not be at the cost of reducing a complex psychological experience that we do not fully understand into a monocular concept with a limited application. Yet, the majority of publications in literary trauma studies utilize the traditional formulation of trauma. For example, Suzette Henke's important book *Shattered Subjects: Trauma and Testimony in Women's Life-Writing* (1998) relies upon the traditional model to discuss the effects of traumatic experience on female identity and autobiographical narratives. The argument relies upon pathological essentialisms of trauma when Henke claims: "There seems to be little doubt that trauma precipitates a violent fragmentation of the (perhaps fantasized) image of the integrated subject" (xvi). Yet, great doubt and debate continue to surround how psychologists and scholars understand the effects of traumatic experience and the cause of dissociation, as I show shortly. Henke later appears to quote Cathy Caruth as a psychological source to define trauma: "Caruth goes on to suggest that the 'experience of trauma repeats itself, exactly and unremittingly' in the form of a mental wound that is 'not available to consciousness until it imposes itself again, repeatedly in the nightmares and repetitive actions of the survivor'" (Henke xviii; Caruth 4). Henke develops a nuanced argument regarding gender, identity, and narrative, but the psychological premise employed to support the argument exerts a reductive view of trauma and consciousness. Moreover, part of the argument appears to be saying that narratives written by women contain specific characteristics due to the fact that females process and express traumatic experience in unique ways. But the argument employs a trauma theory that asserts the opposite: that people respond to trauma in universally similar ways, regardless of individual or cultural variants and regardless of sex and gender.

A more recent publication that demonstrates the dominant model of trauma but that exhibits a broader application and approach is found in Paul Outka's well-written book *Race and Nature* (2008). Outka argues for a theoretical parallelism between Kantian sublimity and Caruthian trauma by employing the traditional model to suggest that "trauma's 'essence' is found in its *failure* to resolve, in the repeated and shattering intrusion of that extrasubjective world into the subject's self-construction" (23). Another example of the employment of the traditional model is Laurie Vickroy's *Trauma and Survival in Contemporary Fiction,* which utilizes the dominant notion that "trauma impairs normal emotional and cognitive responses and brings lasting psychic disruption" to forward her argument (xii).

These works use psychological concepts of trauma as a method of interpretation, but literary trauma theory must be rocked from its thus far immovable traditional pathological foundations. James Berger reminds us in his book *After the End* that trauma theory is a tool for analysis and as such it must "intersect with other critical vocabularies which problematize representation" (573). Although scholar Dominick LaCapra provides important insights regarding the uses of trauma theory in the humanities, he still asserts a traditional conceptualization that emphasizes the pathological and infectious qualities of traumatic experience. LaCapra argues: "Trauma is a disruptive experience that disarticulates the self and creates *holes in existence;* it has belated effects that are controlled only with difficulty and perhaps never fully mastered" (2001: 41, italics mine). A pathological model is implied because the effects of trauma are defined as creating "holes in existence," and by claiming that a traumatic experience can never be known or "fully mastered." Responses to a traumatic experience are universalized to a single component—ontological void. LaCapra's perspective assumes that the self must be verbal in order to be known, therefore implying that identity is binarily constructed based upon speech. A study that employs the traditional model should not be discounted, for it often supplies significant insights into the topic. But the uncritical gaze of trauma in literary criticism, the idea that in order to qualify as trauma the experience or representation must destroy knowledge, needs revision.[12]

There are few publications on the topic of trauma in literature that critique the traditional model. One such book is Amy Hungerford's *The Holocaust of Texts: Genocide, Literature, and Personification* (2003), which problematizes the dominant concept of trauma at use in literary trauma theory and in particular criticizes the notion of transhistorical trauma. However, Hungerford assumes that the traditional model is the only formulation of a literary trauma theory in sections of her argument such as the following: "How can the children of survivors be survivors themselves? Trauma theory—as articulated by both literary critics and clinical psychologists—has provided the answer, the technology by which the trauma of the Holocaust can be transmitted between persons" (92). Hungerford is right in questioning the concept of tranhistorical trauma which is derived from the theoretical foundations of the traditional model, but her argument presumes that psychological trauma theory only offers this formulation. An important book that takes a critical view of the traditional model is Naomi Mandel's *Against the Unspeakable* (2006). Mandel insightfully argues that the dominant discourse of literary trauma theory commits an error by idolizing the unspeakable, which creates a paradigm in which "the 'unspeakable' has already happened and is somehow 'out there,' an independent if amorphous presence, somewhat detached from the culture that produced it and that posits itself in its wake" (4). Another significant scholar who has written about trauma is Geoffrey Hartman. Although Hartman upholds a position primarily of the traditional model in his article "On Traumatic Knowledge and Literary Studies," his analysis of trauma in literature is careful enough to avoid drawing dichotomies. He labels trauma as a negative moment. Although he suggests the main tension is found between the traumatic event and traumatic memory, a standard line of the traditional model, he suggests this is a tension of a "perpetual troping" of experience and memory (538). This type of analysis allows room for a broader interpretation and application of literary trauma theory, yet the discourse of the pathological and unrepresentable still dominates literary criticism.

The prevailing theoretical model that conceptualizes trauma as unrepresentable, an event that intrinsically fragments consciousness and erases knowledge, relies upon a view of memory as veridical recall in which all experiences are exactly recorded and stored in the mind. The view of memory as a warehouse of exactly recorded experience in which the traumatic memory must be retrieved and narrated to another in order to recover is especially problematic when analyzing literature because it privileges the view that all emotional responses to a traumatic event are similar and primarily pathological. This position ignores the plethora of responses to traumatic experiences and avoids the textual implications that the meaning and memory of trauma are contingent upon an assortment of factors.

Moreover, the concept of memory as a warehouse supports the prescription for the talking cure and abreaction found within the traditional model because narration can access the warehouse and undo the negative symptoms. For Leys, the notion of the "unspeakable" memory suggests that the experience, due to its literality, exists as a "pristine and timeless historical truth undistorted or uncontaminated by subjective meaning, personal cognitive schemes, psychosocial factors, or unconscious symbolic elaboration," further emphasizing the memory-as-storehouse schemata in this model (7). However, literary representations diverge from this view and even propose other models of recovery that indicate the individual understands trauma through various actions and rituals that do not necessarily involve speech. Importantly, novels show a spectrum of different types of trauma and acts of remembering that produces a specific articulation of trauma in which the response to a traumatic event may or may not produce pathology.

The pluralistic model allows a view of trauma indicating that in addition to the trope of fragmentation, trauma may disrupt previous formulations of the self and world and involve a reordering of perception, a process that does not necessarily produce an epistemological void. In the novels discussed in the following chapters, an extreme experience can challenge previous formulations of the self and a sense of an integrated identity without inherently carrying an infectious pathological value. In particular, novels show a complex and often contradictory view of trauma and memory, rather than only demonstrating that the remembrance of a trauma is a single, fixed memory that revisits the protagonist in a reduplicative form in flashbacks or nightmares. For example, a novel such as Edward Abbey's *Black Sun* (1971) demonstrates that the protagonist's relation to a particular landscape and community formulates his response to the traumatic experience of losing his beloved. In contrast to showing a reduplicative and unchanging traumatic memory, Abbey's novel portrays a mutable memory that is actively revised over time. The traumatic event itself and the process of remembering reorganize previous perceptions of self in relation to society and in relation to the natural world. The effects of trauma are expressed through the protagonist's multiple memories of his beloved and the traumatic moment that he continues to revise each time he remembers. The different types of memories attached to the event show that memories are malleable to alteration and even invention by the protagonist. Cao's novel also demonstrates that the traumatized protagonist has multiple, contradictory memories of the event, memories which are under continual revision.

Novels demonstrate that extreme experiences may produce a change in perception in response to a violent, disordered event caused by a disturbed individual or society, but texts do not unequivocally portray the protagonist as pathologically divided or as having "holes" in his existence. Suffering caused by traumatic events offers the opportunity to construct new meaning or reformulate consciousness to the extent that the protagonist is not simply viewed as infected or transporting a diseased self to others. In fact, many fictional representations portray the traumatized protagonist as someone who has special knowledge or unique, positive powers that can help others, such as the protagonist Tayo in Leslie Marmon Silko's novel *Ceremony* who becomes a visionary messenger-healer. Tayo recovers from his traumatic war experience after returning home from combat in World War II only by viewing the traumatic events through cross-cultural viewpoints and by coming into physical contact with the land, which allows him to understand the larger bicultural context of his individual experience. He can begin to recover only after he takes part in a Navajo sandpainting ceremony and other rituals, during which Tayo never verbalizes his war experience but performs ritual physical actions. Rituals and physical contact with the land allow Tayo to understand his emotional pain within a larger social context that includes acknowledging the repercussions of war and racial prejudice that he has directly experienced. Importantly, the protagonist recovers not through verbal recall or a trauma narrative but through interactions with the landscape, suggesting that the "talking cure" is not the only avenue to understand the traumatic experience. Other fictional examples that show the traumatized protagonist with unique attributes or special powers include Billy Pilgrim in Kurt Vonnegut's *Slaughterhouse-Five* (1969), who can time travel, or Jebro in Robert Barclay's *Melal* (2001), who is born with an extra finger due to radiation contamination and has special communication abilities with supranatural figures.

Some psychologists have pointed out the failures of the "talking cure" for recovery because it is a Eurocentric concept based on a view of memory as a storehouse that applies poorly when treating non-European or non-Western cultures. Psychologist Derek Summerfield notes that the use of talk therapy is based on Western concepts of the person as a "distinct and independent individual . . . in relative isolation from social context" (24). Summerfield argues that people who have had a traumatic experience require validation of what they have endured. Recovery therefore depends less on obsessive return to the traumatic memory through narrative recall or talk therapy, but more upon reconstructing social and economic networks. Summerfield's research indicates that the modern notion that "traumatic experience is better dealt with if thoughts and feelings associated with it are ventilated, often in a professional setting," has only recently been practiced by the general public and almost exclusively in Western countries (24). It also appears that the thrust of clinical psychology's application of the talking cure requires that a certain locus of power and authority remain in the hands of the therapist, who provides a diagnosis and treatment that function within a western European framework of pathology. Importantly, models of identity and memory that attach a restricted sense of the relational aspects of subjectivity fail to recognize the importance of cultural and social traditions that influence the emotional response to a traumatic experience. Summerfield points out that Western psychology's view of "pathological" responses to trauma, often categorized under the *DSM-IV*'s label of posttraumatic stress disorder, depends upon a worldview of the self as autonomous and individuated:

> Underlying the concept of PTSD is the assumption that the essence of human experience of war and atrocity can be captured by negative psychological effects as they are understood and categorized in the West, to be elicited in the mental life of each individual victim. This view of trauma as an individual-centered event bound to soma or psyche is in line with the tradition in this century in both Western biomedicine and Western psychoanalysis regarding the single human being as the basic unit of study. (18)

Considering views of trauma beyond Western paradigms according to Summerfield would include a notion of both individual identity and the individual experience of trauma, especially exposure to war or a natural disaster, as situated within a social setting, which therefore influences the multiple levels of meaning of the experience. This perspective does not imply that the contextual factors of an individual's experience cause everyone to respond in the same way. Rather, attention to the contextual factors of place and social setting allows for a greater understanding of how traumatic events arise and what socio-political factors may have produced particular events.

The pluralistic model acknowledges the view that different types of traumas produce different responses, often portrayed in the novel as a result of the social valuation of the experience. Novels that represent an active, flexible traumatic memory that is altered in the act of remembering often situate memory within cultural contexts. Remembering the past event can be a significant action in the novel, but memory of the event is not necessarily portrayed as fixed. In certain novels, in each act of remembering the protagonist manipulates the memory of the traumatic experience in ways that alter its meaning.

The novels in this study show a wide range of variability regarding the importance of a verbal reconstruction of the traumatic event and the importance of memory. An example from Cao's novel *Monkey Bridge* demonstrates the contingency of trauma and the variabilities of remembering, a view that upsets the traditional model that claims trauma is universally pathological and that memory is a photographic record of experience. The novel indicates that traumatic experience is as much influenced by social narratives as it is by personal character traits. Both the mother and daughter characters in Cao's novel experience war, but each responds differently to the experience according to individual variants and connection or disconnection to a chosen community—rural Vietnamese or urban Saigon, the ethnic community in Virginia or a mainstream European American group. The mother character deals with the traumatic past based upon her particular traumatic experience, as well as her relationship to her family and national culture, both of which carry mythic notions of identity that direct the comprehension of her sense of self. Remembering in this novel is thus an active process of creation and revision, not a process of reproduction.

What trauma means in literature and how it is valued depends upon the conceptualization of memory because if remembering is an imaginative reconstruction rather than a reduplicative action, then a person's traumatic memory is shaped as much by the present as it is by the past. Therefore, notions regarding the function of memory influence the concept of trauma and the practice of a literary trauma theory.[13] If memory is a fluid process, not static, then it can be actively rearranged according to the needs of the individual at a particular moment, and factors such as personality traits, culture, place, family, or political climate all affect remembering. Viewing the process of remembering as an act of imagination and revision indicates that one's experience of trauma is open to reevaluation as time elapses and is influenced by the audience and context. This upends the traditional model that declares traumatic events are forever imprinted in an exact, absolute, and unalterable form in the brain. In his study *Remembering: A Study in Experimental and Social Psychology* (1932), psychologist Frederic Bartlett argues that memory is a constructive process, not a reduplicative action that merely reproduces past events (204). He rejects the idea that there remains a "memory trace" of every event in the life of an individual (15). Bartlett demonstrates the view that memory is formed by the "interplay" of personal, social, and historical factors:

> Remembering is not the re-excitation of innumerable fixed, lifeless and fragmentary traces. It is an imaginative reconstruction, or construction, built out of the relation of our attitude towards a whole active mass of organised past reactions or experiences, and to a little outstanding detail which commonly appears in image or in language form. It is thus hardly ever really exact, even in the most rudimentary cases of rote recapitulation, and it is not at all important that it should be so. (213)

Bartlett demonstrates that remembering a past event is a process in which what is recalled is actively created in the moment. He demonstrates that "what is initially outstanding [in verbal recall addressed to another] and what is subsequently remembered are, at every age, in every group, and with nearly every variety of topic, largely the outcome of tendencies, interests, and facts that have had some value stamped upon them by society" (254). Defining memory along these lines, Bartlett offers a substantially different concept of memory which informs part of the theoretical foundations of the group of theories and models that define a pluralistic model.

Bartlett's viewpoint would not accept the claim that certain past events are "encoded" in the brain differently than others because remembering the past is contingent on social contexts and, importantly, remembering is a process of "condensation, elaboration, and invention" (205). In contrast to Janet, Bartlett does not believe in the notion of memory as a "storehouse" or "a place where things are put in the hope that they may be found again when they are wanted exactly as they were when first stored away" (200). He would also disagree with the idea that one's complete past experience could become available for reliving, as advocated by the traditional abreactive model.

Bartlett's theories on remembering give rise to a new perspective on how trauma impacts consciousness and memory. Accepting a view of memory as inherently reconstructive leads to different claims regarding how traumatic events are experienced because this view suggests that the meaning of trauma is influenced by different demands placed on the individual, including internal factors of one's personality traits and external factors of place and culture. This model of memory therefore annuls the very idea of traumatic experience that destroys identity because it reveals the recursive process of memory that shapes a relational sense of self. Instead of opposing the traditional model, this view suggests that trauma is multiply interpreted and informed. As such, an inherent pathology is hard to fix permanently or universally to trauma.

In contrast to the model in which memories are conceptualized as "snapshots" that persist unchanged throughout one's life, alternative models conceptualize memory as functioning with "great plasticity" or view memory as a "hypostatization" of diverse processes (Kirmayer 175; Bartlett 201). Psychiatrist Laurence Kirmayer cleverly describes a Bartlettian model of memory when he writes:

> Memory is anything but a photographic record of experience;
> it is a roadway full of potholes, badly in need of repair, worked
> on day and night by revisionist crews. What is registered is
> highly selective and thoroughly transformed by interpreta-
> tion and semantic encoding at the moment of experience.
> What can be veridically recalled is limited and routinely recon-
> structed to fit models of what might have—*must* have—hap-
> pened. (176, author's italics)

This perspective of memory argues against the view that certain memories (traumatic) are "stored" differently than other memories. Kirmayer's model indicates that *all* memories are subject to reconstruction because invention and imagination play a large part in what is remembered and how the past is narrated:

> The effects of imagination on reconstruction and recall are
> pervasive. The tendency to underestimate this—and so to treat
> ordinary memory as veridical recall—probably reflects a more
> general tendency in contemporary Western culture to under-

estimate (and to pathologize) the role of imagination in nor-mal psychological development. (177)

Kirmayer argues that "telling a story of trauma or reliving it occurs in a larger matrix of narrative and social praxis" (181). Accordingly, cultural models of loss and suffering exert a powerful influence on how an individual narrates the past internally to one's self and/or to others. It follows that how a traumatic event is remembered elicits particular responses to the past and influences the individual's conceptualization of the event's impact. If remembering involves invention, then there is no veridical truth or frozen experience "missing" that creates a void in experience or knowledge of the past (traumatic) event.

Bartlett and Kirmayer's model of memory is echoed by psychologist Craig Piers, who examines how individual character traits influence the recall of a traumatic event. Piers demonstrates that memory is influenced by multiple factors such as "mood, preexisting knowledge, contextual cues, encoding strategies, the quality of retrieval cues, contemporaneous efforts to create a coherent sense of self across time, and character style" (61). Piers does not accept the model of trauma provided by van der Kolk that views traumatic events as "self-contained, autonomous 'mental models'" that are set in motion "independent of mediation or control" (60). For to accept this model, one would then believe that traumatic reactions in the past can be transported in whole form to the present and thus determine a person's behavior, especially symptomatic behavior. The abreactive model of trauma also has the tendency to imagine the individual as a passive subject on whom external events are stamped, yet the subject maintains the ability to unconsciously transmit traumatic experiences to others. But Piers offers a view of individual identity as a cumulative and active process in which the meaning of the past changes over time based upon the needs of an active subject.

Claiming that multiple factors influence how an individual interprets a memory of a traumatic event draws attention to the dynamics of identity and frames of reference that assign significance to the traumatic past. Psychiatrist Colin Ross, who runs the Ross Institute for Psychological Trauma, a psychiatric hospital in Texas, shows that traumatic experience and responses are dependent upon a variety of traits and individual factors because memory is not a photographic record. Ross rejects the emphasis placed on abreaction and decentralizes the importance of the traumatic memory: "Trauma therapy is not focused on memory content" because the person can hide within the content of their memories in order to avoid their grief (246). For this practiced psychiatrist, healing from trauma depends more upon addressing the current feelings and behaviors of the individual and less upon the memory of the event or abreaction.[14] Ross argues that abreaction should not be the focus of trauma therapy and healing. Instead, the goal of treatment for a range of psychiatric symptoms and behaviors such as posttraumatic stress disorder, depression, suicide ideation, anxiety, dissociation, schizophrenia, and substance abuse is to "build healthier and more adaptive coping strategies in the individual, not to erase the diagnosis" (232). He says that "the treatment is always for the person as a whole . . . and is not for the diagnosis. . . . Treat the patient, not the diagnosis" (232–33). Perspectives on trauma such as this radically shift the popular literary critical focus beyond the naive view of remembering as a reduplicative process and the special emphasis given to abreaction and narration of the traumatic past that is endemic in literary trauma studies today.

Rather than claiming that all traumatic experiences are frozen in mental limbo and unintegrated, both Ross and Piers argue that multiple factors of an individual's mode of functioning *in the present* influence how a person relates to a traumatic event, further suggesting that the individual can alter the initial meaning of the experience. For Piers, a variety of factors influence remembering, such as the individual's frame of reference—a term that refers to idiosyncratic character traits and the shifting social contexts each time a person remembers.

Piers demonstrates that the influence of "character" in the individual's frame of reference is a highly significant factor in the process of recalling a traumatic event. Character is defined as "a tension-organizing and anxiety-forestalling dynamic system that constitutes an individual's particular perspective, frame of reference, 'mode of existence,' or 'style'" (58). This model resists the binary paradigm that accompanies the traditional model because identity is understood as a dynamic system informed by multiple stimuli, including social spheres of action.

Thus, what Piers calls the "characterological aspects" of individuals, or the diverse factors that organize identity itself, influence one's current response to a traumatic experience. In his model, the attempt to retrieve and reconstruct the traumatic event is less important than understanding how the individual organizes and relates to the event in the present moment of recall. Piers argues:

> One's view of psychopathology, in turn, informs psychotherapeutic technique. For instance, when dissociation theorists link psychopathology to a structural deficit caused by the isolation and encapsulation of a traumagenic pathogen, a historical, reconstructive, and abreactive approach to treatment makes sense. When psychopathology is linked to the ongoing workings of character, the therapeutic attitude and view of change are different. (59)

This perspective highlights a major difference between the traditional and pluralistic models. In a pluralistic framework the response to a traumatic experience is not automatically labeled pathological since the process of remembering is not under the control of the traumatic event itself but available to be influenced by current factors, such as the individual's needs, character traits, and the social context of telling. In Piers's model, the value attached to the experience is created and ascribed in each instance that a person remembers. Therefore, it is not necessary for the person to abreact the traumatic past in order to integrate it because the past is constantly informed by the present-day needs of the individual and her or his social context.

In considering the influence of idiosyncratic character traits on the process of remembering, the concept of identity is equally significant. Taking a longer view of identity in the late-modern period, Paul Wachtel argues that the concept of the modern self has shifted from "bounded, masterful and subjective" to the self as "empty and fragmented" (46). To varying degrees, Wachtel argues that conceptions of self have oscillated between embeddedness and isolation throughout history, but much less attention has been given to the ways that identity "has evolved throughout the life span in relation to the world around us" (47). Instead of imagining the self as isolated, the concept of a relational identity allows for the influence of external pressures as well as internal, individual character traits, all of which significantly shape the action of remembering. Moreover, viewing the self as relational directs attention to the contextual factors of trauma and remembering.

The concept of a relational self can be found in novels wherein even the most isolated character who struggles with a traumatic past is in the process of reformulating his identity in relation to society or a particular place. For example, the protagonist in *Black Sun* is sequestered in his fire lookout tower in the wilderness, but comes into contact with his friend Ballantine through an exchange of letters and infrequent personal visits. These social interactions with Ballantine, along with Will's internal musings on poetic figures of love and loss, provide the protagonist with social models to comprehend his feelings and disorienting change of consciousness. In Barclay's novel *Melal*, the protagonists are situated in relation to family life and social life, both the hegemonic and oppressed cultures, in addition to the supernatural world. Models of identity with a restricted sense of the relational aspects of subjectivity fail to recognize the importance of cultural and social traditions that influence trauma's effects on the self and remembering.

Conceptualizing remembering as an interactive process of constantly revised ideas and feelings, or perceiving remembering as an action influenced by personality traits and social contexts, transforms the way trauma is theorized in literary studies. If memory, like identity, maintains great plasticity, then continual retrieval and recitation of the traumatic event is of less importance than focusing on the present effects of the event and how the meaning of the event might be attributed in each act of remembering or retelling. The idea that trauma pathologizes identity in literary studies is perhaps more a representation that is driven by our contemporary social narratives that encourage this view to be articulated. Although trauma may disrupt an individual's sense of an integrated self, a variety of theories indicate that traumatic experience is not dichotomously locked in a separate area of the brain where it can return on its own desire to terrorize the passive victim or "carrier" of the disease. The direct causality between a traumatic event and pathologic dissociation is based upon the idea that there exists a structural deformation caused by an extreme experience that inhibits recall and induces symptomatic behavior. In addition, the theoretical orientation of the traditional model often portrays the subject who experiences traumatic responses as a "passive receptacle of psychopathological phenomena that can be adjusted 'present' or 'absent'" (Summerfield 18). However, if this view is not taken as the definitive or only model of trauma, then it becomes difficult to claim that traumatic experience pathologically dissociates the self.

Cultivating a plurality of psychological theories, especially those that offer non-dominant views on trauma and memory, allows greater versatility for scholars interested in exploring the varied representations of trauma in literature. In particular, the model of memory as an active process in which remembering is situated in relation to contextual factors affords a wider range of interpretations when deciphering the diverse imagery of trauma in novels. Moreover, pluralistic models elucidate significant aspects of trauma that otherwise would be ignored, such as the representations of suffering that function beyond a framework that insists upon the subject's fragmentation.

Noting the many distinctions in the portrayals of emotional responses to trauma underscores the representational variance in literature. For example, novels do not universally represent trauma as an experience that fundamentally destroys identity. One finds endless examples of traumatic experience expressed in a number of ways that include causing a mental disease, producing a non-pathological transformation of perception, or creating a transcendental feeling, among other representations. Regardless of the positive, neutral, negative, or ambiguous value ascribed to an extreme experience and its remembrance, a traumatic response is an event that propels the plot and emotional action of the narrative to a state wherein the protagonist contemplates new ways of knowing the self and world. The new knowledge may create a perspective of the world that views the self and/or world as sick, diseased, balanced, redeemed, resilient, transcendent, or mystical. Roberta Culbertson argues that narratives may represent the moment of harm as a "supranormal, nonordinary, or mystical experience" that occurs at the level of the body, as seen for example in the novels of Lan Cao and Leslie Marmon Silko (176). A novel often demonstrates that how the protagonist views the self before and after the traumatic event depends upon the type of traumatic event as well as the available narrative formula-tions and social values that are provided by the protagonist's society in the world of the novel.

Psychological models that propose remembering is a flexible, re-lational, and revisionary process call for a careful examination of the contextual factors and social dimensions of traumatic experience and memory in literary portrayals. Contextual factors of trauma in a novel, for example, are expressed through a variety of ways, including but not limited to the protagonist's culture, social class, nation, gender, ethnic-ity, family, and relation to a particular place. The significance of place takes on greater importance in a pluralistic framework because place is a multifaceted medium that portrays the value of trauma. The places of traumatic experience and moments of remembering are significant indicators in describing the value of trauma in a novel because a geo-graphic place contains personal and cultural directives that influence the expression of loss, pain, belonging, and healing. The physical envi-ronment offers the opportunity to examine both the personal and cul-tural histories imbedded in landscapes that define the character's iden-tity and the meaning of the traumatic experience.

Importantly, place functions on symbolic levels because it contains and carries forth layers of meaning that influence the protagonist's com-prehension of suffering. Lang suggests that "the physical environment is often understood best as a symbol that represents cultural values and perceptions invested in a place" (85). The symbolic import of place ex-tends the function of trauma in the novel by including a spectrum of connotations and values. Marina Shauffler argues that "rather than be-ing a static, material construct, place represents a dynamic dance of in-terrelated beings" (101). A specific type of place description, a natural landscape, can be especially prominent in conveying numerous inter-nal and external factors that influence experience and remembering. In *Monkey Bridge,* the mother survives a bombing during Vietnam's civil war and retains a burn scar on her face from the experience, but in an attempt to erase this history, tells her daughter that the scar was caused by a kitchen stove accident. In trauma's remembrance in the novel, the protagonist recalls particular places that contain cultural models of identity and loss that shape her story of what happened or what should have happened to cause her disfigurement. The protagonist revises the memory of what caused the scar, both for herself and to protect her daughter from knowing the actual events, by situating the conflicting memories of the past in relation to the rural lands of the Mekong Delta where she grew up and where she was injured.

When the novel's protagonist imagines that a stove fire caused her facial scar, rather than the actual event, she imagines an ideal past and identity that are rooted in a peaceful setting of robust agricultural fields, which therefore elides her wartime experience. Considering how she would explain the rural landscape where she was injured to her daughter, Thanh says: "I would tell her about a rice field—its beauty, the way it meanders across the land and carpets the horizon in a bright emerald, the way the slate-blue water along the banks buoys the earth and makes it float toward the sky" (172). Descriptions of the land with its mythic symbolism convey how the protagonist relates to herself and imagines the past. The beauty of the field in the revised memory of the past contains the feeling of harmony that the protagonist employs to represent a self that has not been injured and therefore functions to substantiate a positive cultural identity situated in the rural landscape. These rural rice fields, imbued with family and mythic stories that direct the comprehension of the past and the articulation of identity, are imagined in contradictory ways by the protagonist who struggles to come to terms with the traumatic experience. Place therefore becomes vital to representations of trauma in this novel because the physical place of suffering and remembrance of loss becomes an identifiable source to explicate the multiple meanings of the event and the specificity of emotional responses.

Novels produce a diverse array of trauma imagery that shows a multiplicity of responses and forms of consciousness, rather than uniformly representing trauma as an everlasting, recurring event or as an experience known only through somatic symptoms. Noticing the distinctions between disruption and pathological dissociation regarding the transformation of consciousness found in literature allows a critical perspective of trauma beyond that of the traditional model that insists upon the subject's fragmentation. A pluralistic model of trauma encourages an interpretation that exceeds a limited binary paradigm that produces an either/or definition of traumatic experience and memory. This expression of the self is socially contingent and connected to a place of inhabitation and meaning, not binarily dependent on a reenactment of a traumatic experience. The protagonist's subjectivity is thus a fluid process located in relation to new realities or new knowledge. The traumatized protagonist can be shown to exist in relation to a coherent view of reality that is necessarily reorganized through a process of reorientation that might be extremely painful.

Certain novels indicate that a traumatic experience disrupts the previous framework of reality and the protagonist must reorganize the self in relation to this new view of reality. The reorientation of the self is often paired with a reevaluation of the protagonist's relation to society and a specific place or landscape, thus expanding the identification between self and world. For example, *Ceremony* portrays the expanded identification of self and the revision of the relationship between self and society that arise from traumatic experience. The protagonist's recovery in the novel depends upon accepting his identity as one that is connected to a specific natural landscape and tribal community, both of which contain stories of his role in human society and mythic reality. Trauma in the novel lurches the protagonist into a profound inquisitive state in which the meaning of the experience and the process of conceptualizing the self and world are meticulously evaluated. The novel demonstrates this process of questioning as the crux of the plot in terms of the (re)construction of personal and social knowledge. The traumatized protagonist's inquiry into previous "truths" of the self or formulations of identity produces a change in consciousness, however painful this might be, taking the protagonist on a transformative journey that does not necessarily provide relief or recovery. Thus, the places of traumatic experience and healing in a novel foreground the social dimensions of the character's individual experience, which shapes the value of the event and its expression. Landscape imagery, in addition to conveying emotional action, functions as a reference point for the organization of subjectivity and knowledge by marking the network relations that highlight the interactions between the past and present, the internal and external.

The Role of Place in Remembering
Lan Cao's *Monkey Bridge*

In Lan Cao's novel *Monkey Bridge* (1997), trauma is a constellation of individual and social forces that convene at a local landscape to generate both the meaning of the experience and the texture of its remembrance. Traumatic experience is situated within the contexts of immigration and social assimilation, creating alternative meanings and states of subjectivity for the protagonists. The novel describes the relationships between a mother, Thanh, and a daughter, Mai, who arrive in the United States in 1975 as Vietnamese refugees, evoking the historical exodus of individuals from Vietnam in this period.[1] The daughter's accounts of Saigon and Virginia are paired with the mother's nostalgic recollections of her homeland written in her diary. Mai's search for the "truth" of her mother's past becomes a search not only for an articulation of her own identity, but also an exploration of the contours of her relationship to her mother. Their relationship is largely influenced by the presence of traumatic experiences in both women's lives, with each responding differently.

In addition to wartime experiences that both characters experience, Thanh is physically wounded by a napalm bomb and experiences a family betrayal that she attempts to erase through her nolstagic journal entries. These entries act as a wished-for narrative of the past, but hide the actual events of Thanh's life. The mother's self-defining narrative is based within her relations to family and native lands, especially establishing the importance of the rice fields of the rural Mekong Delta in defining her identity. It is the landscape of the past, the land of the traumatic experience, that finally explains the mystery of her past and her father's disappearance.

The mother's diary is the contested site that formulates the past for both mother and daughter. The diary records her childhood in Ba Xuyen, a rural village in the Mekong Delta, and her father Baba Quan, who was a farmer and later secretly becomes a soldier for the communist forces of the north (5). His contradictory representations by Thanh in her diary as both a moral and a corrupt person hide a larger truth of Thanh's wartime experience.

As the U.S. intervention in Vietnam's civil war escalates, Thanh returns to her village to take care of her parents. They are forced to live in a military compound, or "strategic hamlet," built by the United States. When Thanh returns to her village, she travels across the "free-fire zone" to bury her mother in a traditional burial ground. Before she can bury the body, she witnesses her father murder a man and discovers his Viet Cong affiliation that contradicts his professed alliance to the South Vietnamese and Americans. The murder disrupts the burial ritual and she is forced to flee from the site of the crime across the fields near the river to the compound. While running to safety, Thanh is hit with a bomb next to the river by military jets in the "free-fire zone."

She flees to America soon after this incident, but her wartime experience along with her father's betrayal produces an unsustainable tension. The protagonist cannot maintain loyalty to her ancestors or land as dictated by the national mythology encapsulated in the betel nut story due to her traumatic experience and forced departure, thus foreclosing any possible redemptive return to her homeland. The disjunction between the past and present is caused by the inability to reconcile on the one hand, mythic notions of a cultural identity defined by inhabitation of native homelands and loyalty to ancestors' spirits, and, on the other hand, a traumatic departure and modern diasporic life in which return to the native land is impossible.

Thanh's ambivalent relationship to her family and nation is mirrored in a national story of duty and loyalty contained in the betel nut myth. The betel nut myth asserts that a person's soul cannot live outside its homeland because one must protect the spirits of ancestors. The human spirit, according to the myth, "can only live in the village land"

(84). The Vietnamese must inhabit the land of their ancestors so that the ancestors' souls achieve eternal life and regeneration (84). The myth describes two brothers and a woman who leave the village only to die next to a river where their souls turn into a limestone boulder, areca tree, and betel nut vine. The tree and the vine wrap around the boulder and survive periods of "infertility and drought" when other vegetation dies (84). Baba Quan explains that the king learns of the story and proclaims: "There is luminous motion that binds family together for eternity" (85). The betel nut becomes a symbol of the "eternal regeneration and devotion" of family and nation (85). When people chew it they think of their family and "the inextricable connections that keep them tied forever" together (85). This myth also conveys a consciousness inflected by moral codes defined through familial and tribal loyalty, which leads toward fertile lands. Mythologies transmit certain cultural ideologies because myths are "stories drawn from society's history that have acquired through persistent usage the power of symbolizing that society's ideology and of dramatizing moral consciousness—with all the complexities and contradictions that consciousness may contain" (Slotkin 5). Each symbol in the myth conveys the ideology of regeneration through family devotion that requires inhabitation of the local lands. The tree produces an abundance of fruit all year regardless of drought, thus representing the possibility of regeneration found in devotion to family, community, and land.

The novel demonstrates that trauma consists of specific losses situated within a particular cultural context and physical environment. The traumatic experience of the mother causes profound pain that leads to suicide. The experience of the same war by the daughter produces a sense of dislocation, but this disruption leads to a reorientation of perception that carries positive and ambiguous attributes, as shown, for example, with Mai entering college at the end of the novel, a prospect she views with excitement and guilt.

For Mai, remembering the past is rendered as a fluid and flexible process. Mai's experience as an immigrant in America is mediated by the disturbing feelings that a lapse of mental vigilance will transport her back to wartime Saigon: "One wrong move . . . and the force of too many things rammed inside my brain. I was already back there, in a military hospital in Saigon. . . . One wrong move and something had tipped one notch too far and everything was pouring inside out, a live current of nervous wires connecting me to disorder, to insanity" (12). The fear of the past interrupts the present with feelings of blindness, discontinuity, and despair. The character imagines that her existence in the United States as an immigrant is temporary and fragile, vulnerable to the memories that threaten to throw her off balance.

The text opens with a scene that shows remembering through narrative dissociation. The moment of remembrance is an active formulation of how to imagine one's origins in order to define one's identity in a new nation. As the daughter walks into an American hospital to visit her mother who is recuperating from a stroke, she suddenly sees Saigon Hospital before her:

> The smell of blood, warm and wet, rose from the floor and settled into the solemn stillness of the hospital air. . . . A scattering of gunshots tore through the plaster walls. . . . It was all coming back, a fury of whiteness rushing against my head with violent percussive rage. . . . I knew I was not in Saigon. . . . It was not 1968 but 1978. Yet I also knew . . . that I would see the quick movements of green camouflage fatigues, and I knew. I knew the medic insignia on his uniform and I knew, I knew what I would see next. His face, not the face before the explosion, but the face after, motionless in a liquefied red that poured from a tangle of delicate veins. (1–2)

The protagonist later explains that the doctor and medical crew were killed by an unexploded grenade in the body of a soldier on the operating table. Her dissociation shows a transformed state of consciousness in which perception shifts quickly between the past and the present, causing an altered sense of reality and identity. The protagonist's disorientation is expressed in a narrative that shifts rapidly between time periods, creating the impression that both scenes are happening simultaneously because normative narrative markers that suggest temporal movement are absent. The past *is* the present. She sees the American flag, hears the Saigon gunshots, looks at the "lush, green lawn," and

sees the bloodied face at the same moment. Mai "feels the sharp, unsub-
dued scent of chemicalized smoke settle" in her nose from the exploded
grenade. It almost becomes inconsequential if she is actually in Saigon
in 1968 or not because it is the response of her mind to these events in
the present moment that disturbs and interrupts her ability to comprehend the present moment (2).

The view of reality maintains a contradictory perspective and establishes a sense of doubled consciousness. The passage is highly imagistic
and contains strong emotional content, yet the narrator maintains an
emotional distance. The lack of feelings expressed by Mai underscores
the dissociative moment where the viewer is portrayed with a doubled
consciousness that allows her to narrate the events that happened to
her while not providing a narrative of her own emotional response. The
protagonist describes the screams of other people, but not her own. She
describes what faces looked like after the explosion, but does not detail
how she feels about witnessing this. Mai revisits the traumatic memory,
but not with her emotions: "It was all coming back, a fury of whiteness rushing against my head with violent percussive rage." The "fury
of whiteness" could be the hospital walls or the memory or a transmu-
tation of both. However, the "violent percussive rage" is experienced as
a physical blow against her head, not an emotion. The rage is not her
own, but the force of the memory "rushing" into her mind's eye. The
protagonist is simultaneously in the middle of the horror, yet curiously
removed from it.

The repetitive stress on knowing ironically suggests that Mai does not
understand the past. In this moment, there exists no absolute claim to
knowledge of the past, present, nor the self. Perception of the world is
split between the bloody Saigon hospital room and the clean "blinding
white" of the American hospital. In effect, the repeated negation creates
a double vision that sees both the present and the past simultaneously.
The past and the present interact to inform the other so that perception is
a composite and the borders between the two disappear. The protagonist
attempts to create an internal narrative which will allow her to rehearse
her proper place in time by situating herself in relation to the external
world: "This is Arlington Hospital, I reminded myself. There . . . was the
evenly paved lot, its perimeters unenclosed by barbed wire or sandbags"

(3). The landscape offers referential points to gauge the knowledge of self and reality. The relation between knowing and not knowing is mediated by the physical environment. By locating the perimeters of the external reality, she hopes to outline the limits of her internal world.

This conceptual orientation of self in which identity is connected to a landscape continues to be expressed throughout the novel in Mai's relationship to the new landscape of America and the previous landscape of Saigon. When Mai leaves Saigon for America she explains,

> When the plane finally launched into the empty sky, I watched myself hang on to the last bit of ground below. From high up in the sky . . . what I could see of the country was already an altered land. The urge to touch it again, even the monochrome expanse of powdery gray, stayed with me throughout the scattering of turbulence and calm. . . . The fear of separation I suddenly understood that day to be a fear as primordial as the fear of death. (97)

This scene exemplifies the moment of loss that continues to inform the character's sense of self in the new nation. The agony of departure and the desire to maintain a connection to her origins is expressed as a wish for physical contact with the land. The fear of separation from the land is an anxiety of losing the self she identifies as entwined with the landscape and culture of Vietnam.

The landscape provides a referential framework for the protagonist to understand the self because the land contains historical and cultural valence. Mai positions her self in relation to the land during her departure from Saigon in order to define the self and explain her loss of culture and community. More than a metaphor for an emotional state, the land is an entity that contains and transmits knowledge of her sense of self. The conceptual orientation of positioning the self in relation to a landscape suggests that identity is formed by and through a relation to place, a view that expands mythological and psychological considerations of identity formation.

The centrality of displacement and loss causes the protagonist to question previous formulations of a cultural identity defined in relation to the landscape of her native or original nation-state. Stuart Hall argues that a cultural identity is based upon connection to and articulation of the past (400). But a sense of the past is under constant revision in order to fit the needs of the diasporic immigrant. Hall suggests that the fluidity of cultural identity accords the "New World" individual the choice to position the self in relation to the past, wherein the "Old World" is largely imagined based on desires for "lost origins" and a wish to "return to the beginning" (402). In the same way that identity is imagined as fluid and flexible, so too the past continues to be shaped by present needs. The articulation of a cultural identity for the traumatized protagonists in the novel occurs through a desire to position the self within a narrative of belonging to a place or places.[2]

In *Monkey Bridge*, the realization of the impossibility of return coincides with the dream of return for the protagonists. This creates the desire to reinvent or forget the past according to present-day needs. The ability to change the past offers new freedom to interpret the self and even change one's "destiny." For example, members of Mai's Vietnamese immigrant community register a new birthday or change their name for better "karma" and for revenge on ex-husbands and landlords.

The American landscape represents a place of political refuge, free from war, yet the land also functions as a reminder of the life she left behind and the limits of her freedom (Ma 46).[3] The sense of cultural dislocation brought about by being a minority in America brings the protagonists to the Vietnamese community called Little Saigon. On the one hand, the Little Saigon community in Virginia provides support to the protagonists who must confront and resist dominant American perceptions of Vietnamese as "backward peasants" and "enemies" (Cao 39). On the other hand, the community also creates "optical illusions" about the past that allow immigrants to re-create their identities through inventing, or in the language of the novel, "rebirthing" the past, which supports a Bartlettian view of remembering as an act of construction (41). Attending to the significance of forgetting for the New World subject, Édouard Glissant argues that the individual faces an "obligation to remake oneself every time on the basis of a series of forgettings" (273). Forgetting and reinvention are strategies to deceive the dominant culture, but they sometimes backfire on the practitioner.

Self-deception and historical revision allow Thanh as an immigrant in the United States to reconstitute her identity and "roam unattached" from her traumatic past. The process of forgetting can also be viewed as a strategy of resistance against assimilation and a sign of freedom to invent one's self again: "There was, after all, something awesome about a truly uncluttered beginning, the complete absence of identity, of history" (41). Mai ironically comments on the power of forgetting and fantasy in the Little Saigon community: "The obsession with optical illusion was something I might have learned from my mother's friends. It became something of a community endeavor, the compulsion to deceive. . . . Little Saigon was the still-tender, broken-off part of the old, old world, and over here so far away from the old country, our ghosts could roam unattached to the old personalities we once inhabited" (39–40).

The urge to establish a new cultural identity for immigrant protagonists in *Monkey Bridge* becomes a contradictory process that involves acts of assimilation to the dominant U.S. culture. The mother and daughter must conform to a new standard of behavior, language, education, and legal rights, thus creating deep conflicts between previous and new standards of knowing the self and the world.[4] Mai remarks: "It was, in many ways, a lesson in what was required to sustain a new identity: it all had to do with being able to adopt a different posture. . . . The process, which was as surprising as a river reversing course and flowing upstream, was easier said than done" (39). The process of "sustaining a new identity" for Mai is a repositioning based on a contradictory awareness that the new world is different, yet one is expected to function outwardly as if no difference exists. Mai explains that she must "adopt a different posture," but this altered position is predicated upon pretending "that the world was the same now as it had been the day before" (42). Similarly, Thanh attempts reinvention of the past by explaining that her facial burn scar from the napalm was a kitchen accident in order to hide the origin of the wound. But reinvention does not work for Thanh in America even though her journal entries offer an imaginative literary revision of her past.

Importantly, Thanh is confronted with an experience that complicates easy assimilation into a culturally normative narrative, thus causing a greater ambivalence about remembering and forgetting. An expression of this ambivalence is found in Thanh's journal entries which demonstrate a disruptive reordering of the conceptualizations of self and society through the recollection of the past. In significant ways, Thanh's writing is a creative act of survival in an attempt to reformulate identity and create a carefully controlled relation with her daughter based on a past without trauma. Revising the past in her journal is an imaginative effort of the mind to change the karmic cycle she believes is at work in her life.

Thanh creates a largely idealistic, though problematic, version of her childhood, marriage, father, and departure from her native land in order to forget the traumatic events that disrupt her connections to family and native land. Thanh depicts herself as a lucky child who was chosen by fortune to live with the landlord, Uncle Khan, and obtain an education. She does not explain until the last letter that her mother was forced to become the landlord's mistress to pay off Baba Quan's debts, and she is the result of this affair. Baba Quan is first depicted as a loving and eccentric farmer, devoted to religious practices and farming. But in the last letter Thanh reveals he was a Viet Cong soldier who created an intricate minefield that crossed their rice paddies to target U.S. soldiers. Also, Thanh represents her marriage in idealistic terms that show her husband as a professor who is well respected before he dies in Saigon from natural causes. She does not explain her disappointment that her academically "liberal" husband still retained traditional concepts of gender roles and did not want her to work outside the home. These reconfigurations of the past, especially regarding her departure from Vietnam, forget the violence and horror Thanh experienced before escaping. The reversal or erasure of events in her diary obscures the trauma. On one hand, this denial or repression alerts readers to the degree of trauma. On the other hand, Thanh's "gorgeous fictional" description of the past is a method to cope with the traumatic events; rather than telling Mai what happened, Thanh attempts to protect her daughter by these fanciful recollections.

The rural areas and rice fields of Ba Xuyen in the Mekong Delta become a "symbolic repository of value" that Thanh imagines through writing in order to reconstruct an idealized past that lacks traumatic events (Marx 20). In order to combat spiritual death caused by disloyalty

to ancestors and homeland, Thanh's diary entries repeatedly return to
the "beauty" of the rural Mekong Delta landscape and especially the rice
fields near Ba Xuyen in an attempt to forget the past. Thanh's last entry
is a letter addressed to Mai in which she writes:

> My daughter, who was born into a country already at war
> and sheltered in Saigon, has never known a rice field and
> the current of grace that runs through it like golden light. . . .
> To know a rice field is to know the soul of Vietnam. . . .
> That's why the war was fought in the rice fields, because it was
> a war for the soul of the country. (172)

The sublime landscape imagery describes a paradisiacal rice field that
reflects the "soul of the country" and in turn Thanh's soul. Similar to
descriptions found in the betel nut story, the land functions as a referent
for conceptualizations of identity as well as allegiance to the nation. The
beauty of the land substantiates an identity rooted in a national, pasto-
ralized, and mythic landscape that precludes trauma. Addressing the
relationship between landscape and identity, Basso argues:

> Landscapes are available in symbolic terms as well, and so
> chiefly through the manifold agencies of speech, they can
> be "detached" from their fixed spatial moorings and trans-
> formed into instruments of thought and vehicles of purposive
> behavior. Thus transformed, landscape and the places that fill
> them become tools for the imagination, expressive means for
> accomplishing verbal deeds, and also, of course, eminently
> portable possessions to which individuals can maintain
> deep and abiding attachments, regardless of where they
> travel. (102)

The rice fields are landscapes that evoke mythic and apocalyptic dimensions of the human condition in wartime, but also symbolize totality,
wholeness, and regeneration. In significant ways, the repeatedly idealized landscapes become a portable possession that Thanh attempts to
use in order to forget her traumatic experience, to reimagine an untrau-

matic past. In this way, landscape is a tool for the imaginative reconstruction of identity in America.

Thanh's idealized landscape imagery conflicts with Mai's remembrance of the countryside as a place that holds national markers that signify the citizen's duty to one's country and the suffering of soldiers to uphold this notion of the nation. The daughter describes driving through the rural regions and seeing the rice fields and working farmers while going to a vacation destination. In particular, the family always stopped to observe a statue of a soldier along the route:

> The soldier honored was a soldier of the Republic of Vietnam
> Armed Forces, of course, and stories about it abounded. My
> father told me that the statue could lift itself out of the ground
> and walk at night. . . . A severely wounded South Vietnamese
> soldier, a survivor of a battlefield massacre, had come to the
> statue one evening and seen hot tears in its eyes. (68)

There is a sacredness and respect reserved for the soldier who has died for the worthy cause of the nation. The military statue in the countryside reminds Mai of the heroism of men and their devotion to their country, but it also acts as a reminder in the novel of the suffering experienced by Thanh, who was also wounded in war. But Thanh exemplifies a different type of soldier who fought to uphold her duties to family and nation and was not given a medal or national marker to commemorate her losses. She experiences shame rather than honor because of the complexity of her cultural and mythological directives.

The journal narrative of the beauty of rural lands acts as a corrective to Thanh's traumatic experience. The protagonist does seem to believe that her spirit belongs in Ba Xuyen, but she cannot accommodate this belief with her war experience. In the last diary entry, Thanh describes the "death of her village soil" and her own near-death experience. The protagonist's description of displacement and survival culminates with the quote below that demonstrates the profound loss induced by trauma:

> What could I have done? A part of me died forever by that
> river's edge, and I have never been able to touch it since, that

most wounded part that still lies inert beyond my grasp, like
the sorrow on my face, seared by fire dropped into the free-
fire zone from a plane as I fled from the cemetery toward the
safety of the boat. Everything was on fire. I will always remember that moment as the moment the earth screamed its tormented scream. From the ground where I was lying face-up, I
could see the gathering red that poured from a lacerated sky,
the red of fire bisected by a black, black smoke as far away as
the untouchable line where heaven meets earth. (250–51)

Thanh's moment of trauma widens the doors of perception to allow a
view of the world and self that reorients previous conceptions. This view
of reality constructs a world that deviates or is not linked at all to the
previous world and its normative value. The ethical borders that guide
human behavior and comprehension are rearranged as the self merges
with the landscape on fire. The wounding of the body is paired with
all other personal, familial, social, and cultural factors. Similar to landscape descriptions of the rice fields in Thanh's earlier diary entries, the
land in this passage functions as the representational medium through
which trauma is conveyed to those who were not there. The apocalyptic
vision of a burning earth mirrors the extent of horror that Thanh feels
but cannot communicate in the first person.

The landscape imagery evokes the betel nut's mythic landscape because like the woman in the myth, Thanh also lies by the riverbank,
close to death. The river is a "character" who plays a central role in the
contemporary traumatic events of the novel: the murder takes place by
the river, Thanh's mother's body is left unburied near the river, and
Thanh is nearly killed by napalm as she enters the river with her boat.
Contrary to the mythic symbolism of the river as a source of regeneration, the river in *Monkey Bridge* is the locus of trauma and death. In contrast to the betel nut myth, the river here does not carry Thanh toward
eternal life or regeneration. Rather, the river is the source that covers up
the act of murder born out, in part, of the class conflict between Baba
Quan as a poor farmer and Uncle Khan as a rich landlord. In addition,
Thanh could not uphold her family duty to bury her mother in ancestral
grounds, causing her mother's soul to move into a "non-earthly, ever-

lasting existence" (247). These events undermine the social symbolisms of the betel nut myth and disrupt notions of family and national loyalty. The novel is a recapitulation of the ancient myth into a modern one, save one large difference: regeneration is unattainable.

In the remembrance of the traumatic event, the protagonist must return to notions of totality and redemption in terms of specific relationships to family, ancestors, and land. But these beliefs or "truths" have been rendered untenable. The experience by the river therefore dismantles the symbology that underlies the creation of a cultural identity found in the betel nut myth, which prevents her from participating in the cultural narrative that defines national and ethnic identity. The inherent connections between family and ancestors promoted by the betel nut myth are precisely the connections that trouble Thanh. The symbolic order of the betel nut myth that positions the individual in relation to family, land, and nation is disrupted by traumatic events, leading to a disoriented perception of world and self. The betel nut mythology of self, land, and nation is shown as an underlying component of how the protagonist remembers the past, but traumatic experience disorders the traditional symbolism that informs identity. The events by the river force the traumatized protagonist to reconsider traditional ideologies of her culture that promise eternal life through devotion to family and inhabitation of native lands. Thanh's experience thus prevents the hope of regeneration and the afterlife found in the myth because trauma disrupts the symbolic order of linguistic meaning and corporeal knowledge.

Furthermore, the protagonist views her experience as a function of karma, which helps consolidate her opinion that she is doomed to be haunted by the terrible past with no ability to change her future. Thanh writes: "Karma is . . . a continuing presence that is as ongoing as Baba Quan's obsession, as indivisible as our notion of time itself" (252). She understands her experience in war as a result of larger imbalances in her native nation's power in the world. When she witnesses her father murder a man and deposit the body in the river, she writes: "There was the legacy that coursed through the landscape like a slow but steady rush of death foretold" (250). Her past, which she calls a legacy of "sin, death, and murder," is a result of karma in her view. Thanh feels that the crime her father committed is an evil force and a betrayal that will haunt her, just as the invasions of other nations in the historical past by her own country will negatively influence her personal life. She writes:

> No one can escape the laws of Karma. Nor can a country di-
> vest itself of the karmic consequences of its own actions . . .
> for every deed of destruction there is a consequence. Karma is
> based less on rights and entitlements than on moral duty and
> obligation, less on celebration of victories than on repentance
> and atonement. (55–56)

The protagonist sees her war experience not only as a result of U.S. intervention, but also as a result of karma due to her people's long military history of invasions, occupations, and revolutions. Although the circumstances in war are a direct result of U.S. involvement, which she acknowledges, she also views her traumatic experience as a result of her government's foreign policies. The consequences of her nation's military actions are placed within a Buddhist paradigm for the protagonist, who views her individul trauma within a larger cultural context.

Traumatic experience is portrayed in the novel from a non-Western perspective that values trauma in terms of personal, global, and even mythic contexts. Although Thanh does not recover through her journal rewriting of the traumatic past, she is not portrayed as pathological. Importantly, the text magnifies the significance of the place of trauma— the natural landscape—in order to situate individual trauma, regardless of how private or solitary the experience, within a larger cultural context and social sphere. Place, therefore, takes on a central role in defining trauma and its value for the characters and communities in the novel. The novel suggests that rather than a transhistorical definition of trauma, the responses to an extreme event are experienced and narrated differently due to individual variants and temporal specificities. Trauma in fiction thus posits a provocative paradigm: the narrative asserts the specificity of trauma while simultaneously making the claim that the protagonist is a representative cultural figure.

The Traumatized Protagonist and Mythic Landscapes
Leslie Marmon Silko's *Ceremony*

Leslie Marmon Silko's novel *Ceremony* (1977) follows the life of Tayo, a mixed-race American Indian who transitions from being a traumatized soldier to a respected storyteller in his Laguna Pueblo community. The protagonist's suffering is portrayed as a result of numerous events, including his combat experience, the deaths of his cousin Rocky and Uncle Josiah, and personal experiences of discrimination based on his ethnic identity. It is also the result of tribal mythic Indian characters who have produced imbalances in contemporary American society. Importantly, the protagonist's trauma is entwined with his relationship to the land and situated within a tribal-mythic narrative that reenacts (and rewrites) Laguna mythic creation stories that position different animal and mythological figures in a battle for the spiritual regeneration of humanity and for the preservation of the earth's fecundity.[1] Initially, traumatic experience alienates the protagonist, but later it provides an avenue for him to occupy a privileged role in the Laguna community as a healer and "messenger" between different ethnic groups in an ailing America. Traumatic events disrupt the protagonist's coherent sense of self, yet importantly these events reformulate his identity by initiating new relationships to his Native and Euro-American societies as well as to the lands of the Southwest.

Working within Laguna, Navajo, and Euro-American worldviews of psychic imbalance and healing, the novel demonstrates that individual trauma is rooted within cultural contexts and specific landscapes. Significantly, the protagonist's struggles are situated within historical frameworks of Indian resistance to colonization to the extent that Tayo becomes a cultural figure who represents the effects of colonization, forced assimilation, and racial discrimination.[2] In many ways, his actions in the novel embody elements of the historical struggle experienced by Indian tribes in the United States to reclaim their land and assert their rights from the sixteenth century until, some would argue, today. On one level, the protagonist's trauma arises from his personal experiences in war. On another level, trauma arises due to the socioeconomic exploitation that is collectively experienced by an ethnic group so categorized by the dominant society. For example, the correlation between the individual and collective experiences of displacement based upon ethnicity is represented in one of several examples when Tayo strives to reclaim Uncle Josiah's Mexican cattle that were stolen by Euro-American ranchers. Tayo's individual intent to reclaim the cattle is presented as a simple desire to finish the job that Josiah had started and take care of "family business." In addition, however, Tayo's actions evoke the collective desire expressed by other tribal members in the novel to reinhabit their land as well as to reassert their rights and a modern, mixed-race tribal identity. Thus, bringing the cattle "home" equally resonates with Tayo's emotional recovery and symbolizes the historical indigenous struggle to reclaim land taken away by European colonizers and their descendants.[3]

Individual trauma is therefore situated in relation to cultural, ecological, and mythological contexts. The novel points out that the cultural context that creates racial hatred and violence is caused by the Indian witch "Destroyers" whose "evil" affects all races and spans ancient, mythic, and modern times (46). The Destroyers do not have a race or culture, but work to sicken and kill all humans (249). War, murder, and racially motivated hate crimes in the novel are part of the witchery or evil that any group or race of people can participate in, as exemplified by the gruesome torture and killing of Harley at the uranium pit mine on the Laguna reservation (250). According to the novel, Indian witchery and its evil began without white people, when "there was nothing European" (133).

To understand the origins of the protagonist's trauma, the novel explores how his unresolved grief continues to disorient his perceptions of self and relation to place when he returns home to his Laguna community after his combat in the Philippines during World War II. When Tayo's unit captures several Japanese soldiers and executes them, Tayo refuses to kill the soldiers because they "looked too familiar" and claims that his Uncle Josiah is standing in the lineup. The narrator explains:

> Tayo could not pull the trigger. The fever made him shiver,
> and the sweat was stinging his eyes and he couldn't see
> clearly; in that instant he saw Josiah standing there; the face
> was dark from the sun, and the eyes were squinting as though
> he were about to smile at Tayo. (7–8)

His cousin Rocky tries to reason with Tayo that Uncle Josiah is not standing with the Japanese soldiers about to be shot, but Tayo is not convinced: "[Tayo] examined the facts and logic again and again, the way Rocky had explained it to him . . . but he could not feel anything except a swelling in his belly, a great swollen grief that was pushing into his throat" (9). Tayo sees Uncle Josiah fall with the Japanese soldiers being shot, revealing his guilt over leaving his uncle alone back home, his special knowledge that Josiah has died at a similar moment on the reservation, and his belief that all humans are connected independent of race or nationality.

The "great swollen grief" is a response to the "evil" of war, a war in which later, after they capture the Japanese soldiers, their unit is captured by a larger Japanese unit. The protagonist and his cousin along with other soldiers are taken as prisoners of war and forced to walk long distances to a prisoner camp. Tayo remembers being captured and forced to walk through the jungle with his cousin dying: "Tayo hated this unending rain as if it were the jungle green rain and not the miles of marching or the Japanese grenade that was killing Rocky" (11). This forced march historically evokes the Japanese military's 1942 Bataan Death March in the Philippines when tens of thousands of American and Filipino prisoners of war were forced to walk about one hundred kilometers to a prison camp with thousands dying along the way.

These are some of the remembered events of war that cause a traumatic response in Tayo, but it is important to note that Tayo's fever and hallucinations began before his capture and his cousin's death. This suggests that Tayo's trauma comes from sources other than war, including society, family, and culture.

In Silko's novel, individual trauma is related to a cultural experience of violence and loss. The novel emphasizes that the protagonist's trauma is caused from more than the war due to his experiences of racial discrimination and childhood poverty. Neglect from some of his family members, primarily his aunt, and intolerance to his mixed-race ancestry from both Indian and white societies contribute to the disruption of the protagonist's cohesive sense of self. As a child Tayo is targeted by Indian boys in school, especially by Emo, because Tayo is "part white" and called a "half-breed" (42). Emo continues to torment Tayo after the war when they both return to Laguna, eventually becoming Tayo's final adversary. Even Tayo's aunt treats him like an outsider due to his mixed ethnicity, telling him she had to "conceal the shame of her younger sister" who was forced to be a prostitute and was not certain of the identity of Tayo's father (29). Before living with this aunt, Tayo lived with his mother near the homeless area under the bridge in a makeshift tent by the river. He would often spend nights at bars in town as a young child waiting for his mother and hiding under the bar tables (109). His aunt continues to ostracize Tayo when he returns home after the war. His aunt disapproves of him even more because now he is sick and she "probes him for new shame" to add onto the original shame of his mixed-race parentage since his father is not Indian (57). The narrator explains:

> Since he could remember, he had known Auntie's shame
> for what his mother had done, and Auntie's shame for him.
> He remembered how the white men who were building
> the new highway through Laguna had pointed at him. . . .
> He understood what it was about white men and Indian
> women: the disgrace of Indian women who went with them.
> And during the war Tayo learned about white women and
> Indian men. (57)

Due to Tayo's own shame from internalized racism arising from his racial hybridity and his aunt's glorified approval of her "full-blooded" son

Rocky, Tayo is confused by the fact that he is alive while Rocky is dead. Tayo thinks to himself: "It was him, Tayo, who had died, but somehow there had been a mistake with the corpses, and somehow his was still unburied" (28). His aunt's disapproval and society's intolerance of his racial hybridity, in addition to witnessing his cousin's wartime death in the jungle of the Philippines, commingle to produce Tayo's grief and silence. On a mythological level, the novel indicates that World War II and racial discrimination are products of Indian witchery by the Destroyers.

After returning from the war, the protagonist refuses to talk while staying at the veterans' hospital in Los Angeles where "white doctors" encourage him to talk by sitting with him in a small white room with a single barred window: "He reached into his mouth and felt his own tongue; it was dry and dead, the carcass of a tiny rodent" (15). He feels exhausted from "fighting off the dreams and voices; he was tired of guarding himself against places and things which evoked the memories" (26). The protagonist is horrified by memories of the past because they are consumed by his war experience, yet his memories are inextricably linked to his past before the war and his relationships to his cousin and uncle to the extent that the two types of memories are interdependent.

Even though Tayo does eventually speak a few words to the doctor, nightmares and flashbacks continue as he returns to the Laguna reservation. There he sees the traditional Laguna medicine man, Ku'oosh, who performs a traditional Laguna healing ceremony that includes storytelling, making it necessary for Tayo to explain his experiences in the "white people's big war" (35). Ku'oosh prompts Tayo to explain what happened to him during the war, emphasizing the importance of storytelling and the use of language that reflects the cultural contexts of each word. Ku'oosh speaks in Laguna to Tayo, explaining: "No word exists alone, and the reason for choosing each word had to be explained with a story about why it must be said this certain way. . . . The story behind each word must be told so that there could be no mistake in the meaning of what had been said" (35–36). But Tayo cannot tell a story because he does not clearly remember or distinguish between his actions and others. Tayo muses that "the old man would not have believed anything so monstrous" as World War II because even Laguna myths did not incorporate such atrocity (37). The protagonist in fact never verbalizes his war experiences, yet he recovers from his traumatic experience through a variety of physical actions and spiritual rituals that locate his identity and remembering process within a cultural context.

Although the protagonist works to understand his traumatic experiences, this understanding can only come about after he contemplates other stories of suffering, both historic and mythic, that help him understand his experiences coherently. The protagonist understands his past only after he performs a ritual with the healer Betonie (in which he does not narrate his war experience), sees the mountain lion, interacts with the mythic nature-figure Ts'eh, reclaims his uncle's cattle, and watches the rain come. The absence of a "talking cure" or the narrative recall of the past by the traumatized protagonist suggests that retelling the traumatic past to another is less important than reconnecting to the land with its human, natural, and mythic histories that help the person reestablish a relationship to the social community of his home.

Silence, ellipsis, and the initial achronological plot emphasize the painful process of remembering and reflect the cultural models available to express the experience, rather than necessarily representing the inherent wordlessness of trauma. The novel challenges the critically popular claim that the traumatized protagonist's muteness represents the psychological fact that the prelinguistic imprint of trauma makes it impossible to narrate the experience. Silence may evoke dissociation or numbness at different points in the narrative, but it is not employed consistently as a shorthand to represent an essential epistemological void caused by an extreme experience. Rather, the protagonist's silence and inability to vocalize the past in this novel is a rhetorical strategy to show emotional suffering, confusion, and, at times, dissociation.

The protagonist's struggle with the past and the resulting disruption of identity is a motif to express a reordering of perception caused by a profound experience. Narrative dissociation is portrayed in several scenes by altering the narrative structure to create a disjunction in the protagonist's coherence of identity and perception of the external world. The narrative shifts abruptly between past and present to demonstrate the alteration of the protagonist's sense of self and relation to others as he remembers his experience as a soldier fighting a war that he doesn't understand.

The protagonist's disorientation and grief continue throughout the novel in a seemingly fragmented narrative with multiple genres and plot lines concerning humans, mythic figures, and ecosystems. Halfway through the novel these fragments are interconnected to reflect a Laguna-Navajo cosmology that highlights a view of the interpenetration of contemporary and mythic realities. The plot structure also reflects, according to Rinda West, a formal innovation of the American Indian novel. West argues that the American Indian novel contains a "cyclical, enmeshed, community-centered, and often oral way of ecological seeing" (xi). Importantly, the underlying interconnections between the disparate parts of the novel can only be viewed once Tayo has achieved a sense of self-realization. In this regard, the disruptiveness of the plot often reflects the traumatized protagonist's altered consciousness. For example, the following narrative dissociation passage exemplifies this in detailing Tayo's visit to the bar with other war veterans:

> The floor was covered with dirty water. It was soaking through his boots. The sensation was sudden and terrifying; he could not get out of the room, and he was afraid he would fall into the stinking dirty water and have to crawl through it, like before, with jungle clouds raining down filthy water that smelled ripe with death. He lunged at the door; he landed on his hands and knees in the dark outside the toilet. The dreams did not wait any more for night; they came out anytime. (56)

The external environment reflects the blurring of boundaries between past and present through a sudden, unexpected alteration of consciousness. Consciousness contains the act of remembering and the act of perceiving the external world in the present moment. Existence becomes split or shared between his forced march as a prisoner in the Philippines and the present moment at a bar in America. The prose embodies the internal movement of thoughts quickly moving from the dirty bathroom water back to the horror of his war experiences and back again to the present moment. The link between the present and the past is the water, but the reader is left to interpret the silence that surrounds exactly what happened in that distant jungle. The integrity of identity is transposed between the violence and fear in the jungle and the present confusion and disgust of the bar. The place in which Tayo remembers reflects his inability to understand his traumatic past: the darkness of the room clouds his vision, the water terrifies him, and he vulnerably falls onto the ground.

As the narrative continues, the protagonist interacts directly with the natural world, thus enabling a comprehension of a coherent self. The relationship to the land is one of both physical contact and an emotional state in which remembering signals an inner coherence rather than disconnection. In the bar he is confused and frightened, but when Tayo inhabits the natural environment he gains a measure of peace:

> In a world of crickets and wind and cottonwood trees he was almost alive again; he was visible. The green waves of dead faces and the screams of the dying that had echoed in his head were buried. The sickness had receded into a shadow behind him, something he saw only out of the corners of his eyes, over his shoulder. . . . The place felt good; he leaned back against the wall until its surface pushed against his backbone solidly. (104)

Contact with the environment allows for a clearer perception and a sense of coherency. Through the experience of nature he is attached to a particular place and feels "visible" now rather than "white smoke." The protagonist locates himself physically just as he begins to locate his trauma in terms of an internal emotional landscape that corresponds with a broader knowledge of his identity situated in a southwestern landscape and reservation community. The protagonist begins to understand his trauma in relation to the landscape so that the horrible war experiences are not forgotten, but placed in a unifying pattern within other culturally informed narratives of Laguna history and mythic battles against evil. In this moment he listens intently to the outside world that affords a perspective of the self in the present moment rather than primarily through remembering the war.

Importantly, greater contact with the desert landscape through the hybridized sandpainting ceremony allows the traumatized protagonist to situate his experiences in terms of personal, cultural, and mythic histories. Both Laguna and Western worldviews are necessary to "see" and narrate the past, along with the integration of individual and community stories connected to a specific Laguna landscape. The hybridized sandpainting ceremony based on Navajo rituals transitions between mythic poetry and modern prose, signifying this movement between modern and mythic time periods. During the ritual, Betonie guides the songs and directs Tayo to perform certain actions, including walking through hoops that represent doorways. In the following passage, the "ritual-mythic" time period in stanza form is combined with the within-the-present, "everyday" period in prose form:

> e-hey-yah-ah-na!
> At the Dark Mountain
> born from the mountain
> moves his hand along the mountain
> I have left the zigzag lightning behind
> I have left the straight lightning behind. . . .
> When he passed through the last hoop
> it wasn't finished
> They spun him around sunwise
> and he recovered
> he stood up
> The rainbows returned him to his
> home, but it wasn't over.
> All kinds of evil were still on him.
> From the last hoop they led him through the doorway. It was
> dark and the sky was bright with stars. The chill touched the
> blood on his head; his arms and legs were shaking. (144)

In this ritual performance, nature acts as both a symbolic metaphor and a physical arena where the individual engages the self and the past. The stanza structure of Betonie's chants places Tayo's modern healing within a Navajo-like sandpainting ritual, combining the boundaries between the two time frames and stylistic forms. Consequently, the healing ritual takes place within a continuous present that spans past, present, and future.

The temporal overlap blurs the two worlds of the mythic and the modern so that Tayo is both an actor and a viewer in the story and ceremony, therefore presenting his trauma and recovery as both an individual and a cultural process. The singer's chants are spoken in the first person for the healing prayers and the story of returning home and healing. Then the narrative shifts suddenly in the last stanza into third person, incorporating Tayo as an actor into the healing chants of the performance. Betonie sings as Tayo walks through the five hoops (rainbows) of the white corn sandpainting with blood running through his hair from the cut inflicted by Betonie with a flint stone, an act that locates pain on the body in order to allow Tayo to return home to the "Dark Mountain." The creation myth in the novel indicates that Laguna people have been born from the earth and their stories of self are inextricably linked with the land. When Betonie speaks of returning to the mountain, he is calling for Tayo to return to the home of the self. The pathway back to "belonging" in the ceremony is also a process of locating one's self in relation to others and to a landscape.

The transition to recover is described in terms of renewal brought about by rain, and this renewal is contrasted to the strike of lightning that anticipates rain. The rebirth of the self is contained within the rebirth of the day as we see the speaker embodied as dew in the early morning light. These stanzas suggest that home and nature are the same so that a return home must contain a reconnection with the geographical setting. On a symbolic-mythic level, the speaker and the participant embody the mountain, wildflower, rain, and sun, indicating that an intimate relationship between human and nonhuman is a necessary process of identity formation. In Silko's essay, "Landscape, History, and the Pueblo Imagination," she argues that for Laguna Pueblo peoples an intimate relationship between human and nonhuman is a necessary process of identity formation:

> The human beings depended upon the aid and charity of the
> animals. Only through interdependence could the human be-

ings survive. . . . Life on the high arid plateau became viable
when the human beings were able to imagine themselves as
sisters and brothers to the badger, antelope, clay, yucca, sun.
Not until they could find a viable relationship to the terrain,
the landscape they found themselves in, could they *emerge*.
(273)

The "viable relationship with the land" in the world of the novel is a process Tayo must enact during the sandpainting ceremony to encourage
his journey back to "happiness" as identified in the ceremonial song.

The protagonist's interactions with the land and nonhuman natural
environment are part of the process of remembering and reconstitut-
ing the self due to the cultural histories that are embedded in the desert landscape. The awareness of relationships between different objects
in the sandpainting ceremony encourages Tayo to imagine and cultivate a relationship with his own emotional landscape and to appreciate
the symbolic cultural values of those objects.[4] In addition, the physical
movement in the ritual connotes health and recovery, in contrast to the
immobile state Tayo experiences after the war. In discussing American
Indian ceremonies, Paula Gunn Allen explains that integration is a central, general feature of ceremonies, even though specific purposes of
ceremonies vary between tribes according to culturally specific contexts:
"The purpose of a ceremony is to integrate: to fuse the individual with
his or her fellows, the community of people with that of other king-
doms, and this larger communal group with the worlds beyond this
one" (62). Valerie Harvey's research on Navajo sandpainting ceremonies demonstrates that the dry painting of the sands and placement of
objects in the sand painting depend on the specific placement and location of symbols in relation to one another (237). The relationship between symbols unifies the whole picture and determines the healing
power of the ritualistic action.

Significantly, identity is imagined and enacted in relation to others,
specifically the land, and the symbolic interactions that occur between
the human and nonhuman point to the broader histories attached to
the place where the ceremony occurs. Direct contact with the land is
part of the protagonist's process of remembering and healing due to

the cultural histories that are connected to the southwestern landscape. Michael Kowalewski argues that "human behavior and ethical deliberations take place within the context of local communities, both human and biotic. Individuals and communities come into consciousness *through*, not apart from, the natural environments they inhabit" (30). Focusing on the concept of place understood in terms of a bioregion, Tom Lynch argues that a bioregion is defined by natural boundaries, not necessarily political boundaries, that take into account political, cultural, and ecological practices to form identity.[5] Identity viewed through an ecological perspective is therefore relational and interactive, dependent upon specific exchanges with the land and the community.

The protagonist begins to understand better his experiences of childhood, war combat, and his present life, suggesting that recovering an integrated sense of identity is possible after traumatic experiences. After the ritual, Tayo looks at the landscape and realizes that "there were no boundaries; the world below and the sandpaintings inside became the same that night" (145). The boundaries or "doorways" between modern and mythic, past and present, blend into a unifying whole as Tayo sees the connections between his individual anguish and the larger cultural legacies of colonization, racial conflict, and World War II. The protagonist realizes that "his sickness was only part of something larger, and his cure would be found only in something great and inclusive of everything" (125–26). The understanding of trauma depends on a cross-cultural perspective of suffering and health situated within the interconnections between cultures and narrative modes.

After the sandpainting ceremony, when the protagonist recovers the lost cattle and brings them home, a moment of correspondence occurs between inner and outer worlds: "He smiled. Inside, his belly was smooth and soft, following the contours of the hills and holding the silence of the snow" (205). Tayo's calmness is reflected in a landscape that is "smooth and soft" with a silence that opens him to an outward listening to the natural world and its mythological components. The sandpainting ritual activity transcends specific cultural traditions by combining knowledge from different cultures to attain a curative power. In this way the novel challenges the traditional model's essentialist perspective on trauma and identity by indicating that the knowledge and value of a traumatic experience are located in the interconnections between cultures and narrative modes that embrace plurality and hybridity rather than a singularity.[6] The protagonist's healing process depends upon incorporating traumatic memories through a physical reconnection to a culturally significant landscape. The greater coherency and integrity of self parallels the protagonist's inhabitation of and interaction with the local landscape and establishing his role as a spiritual messenger for the Laguna community. Just as the shape of the narrative around the silence of dissociation may provide information about the relationship the individual maintains with a traumatic experience, so too the quality of the interaction between Tayo and the landscape with its mythic figures reveals the protagonist's ability to comprehend the traumatic past and situate himself in the present.

Acknowledging a concept of trauma beyond the traditional model suggests a view of trauma as relational and positioned within a social setting that is framed by a specific culture, historical period, geographic place, and community. In this novel the protagonist participates in other ceremonies in addition to the major sandpainting ritual that draw him into contact with the local physical environment, such as hunting rituals for the mountain lion and prayers with the mythic woman Ts'eh when they gather flowers and repaint the pregnant she-elk at the base of the sandstone cliff in hopes of receiving rain and spiritual regeneration. Cultivating a relationship to the land plays an essential role in Tayo's healing because the sky, rain, mountain, and desert represent parts of the mythic reality and cultural landscape in which he must situate himself in order to tell his story. The natural world is central to the process of understanding trauma by affording a place to engage the process of remembering, thus creating a meaningful internal emotional landscape.

Moreover, the coherence of identity and memory is achieved through a collaboration of cross-cultural worldviews that create new ways of comprehending and representing traumatic events. When Tayo engages the elders in the kiva holding the role of a spiritual messenger, he places himself in the tribal community's narrative with a history that acknowledges mythological aspects to experience and remembering. The lack of a narrative about his war experience to others does not prevent his regaining a coherent sense of self, for he is able to understand the traumatic event and integrate the previously disparate parts of his past through interactions with nature that carry mythological significance that aid in his healing. The traumatized protagonist must first immerse himself within a familiar natural landscape that contains cultural stories of loss and recovery in order to decipher the meaning of his experience. The novel thus demonstrates that a specific cultural context and place shapes the expression of trauma and the value of its remembrance.

Wilderness, Loss, and Cultural Contexts
in Edward Abbey's *Black Sun*

Edward Abbey's novel *Black Sun* (1971) takes place in the American Southwest high desert region where the protagonist experiences and remembers trauma, demonstrating that the reframing of subjectivity occurs through an exploration of the self in relation to the process of remembering and inhabitation of the wilderness. *Black Sun* is one of the most structurally unusual novels of Abbey's career, and perhaps for this reason it has been overlooked by critics, who tend to focus on more popular texts such as the novel *The Monkey Wrench Gang* or the environmental treatise *Desert Solitaire*. The achronological plot with its allusions and parodies of Renaissance poetry, especially sonnets by Thomas Wyatt, shows a reliance upon cultural models of love and loss found within a Renaissance humanistic discourse in order to explore how trauma alters subjectivity. Similar to the novels discussed earlier, *Black Sun* examines the transformation of consciousness caused by a traumatic experience. This novel suggests that trauma reorganizes previous formulations of the self by contextualizing this perceptual reorientation in terms of English literary traditions as well as an American southwestern landscape.

In the novel, the protagonist Will Gatlin is a forest fire ranger near the Grand Canyon during the 1960s whose girlfriend, Sandy, disappears one day never to return. The protagonist suspects that she died on a solo hike into the canyon, but there is never a definitive answer to her disappearance even six years later when the novel begins. The narrator explains the protagonist's despair: "He felt the pang of loss, the bewildering pain of something precious, beautiful, irreplaceable swept away forever" (144). The traumatic loss is unresolved, and memories that in the past were pleasant now return to create a painful existence. Will, referred to mostly in the narrative as Gatlin, ruminates after Sandy's disappearance as he paces his "catwalk" or balcony around the tower: "What is this thing that haunts my soul night after night and day after day, week after month after year? . . . I see her dancing again in the candlelight . . . her black skirt twirling around her. Hair flying, eyes shining, arm outstretched" (98). Remembering Sandy is a burden because he is unable to accept her death, labeling his seemingly illogical feelings as absurd because the feeling of loss is consuming.

The achronological plot is composed of the protagonist's memories of first meeting Sandy, their romance, her disappearance, his descent into the canyon in search of her where he comes close to death, his departure from the fire lookout tower, and his return back to an urban center. The first and last chapters end with Gatlin looking out over the forest in silence: "Each time he looks out upon this world, it seems to him more alien and dreamlike than before. And, all of it, utterly empty" (15). The external world is unfamiliar and foreboding for the protagonist in his current state of suffering where he is confronted with a sense of empty meaning. The last chapter ends with Gatlin staring "out the window, into the forest," unresponsive to questions from his friend, Ballantine (157). Remembering his relationship with Sandy is juxtaposed to contemporary solitary musings in his wilderness fire lookout tower and interactions with Ballantine. The unexpected loss of his beloved forces the protagonist into a state of silence that involves a profound listening to the external world. The narrative disruption of time and the emphasis on the character's silence are formal devices to represent the process of remembering and its influence on consciousness. The interruptive experience of time represents the action of remembering as a creation of knowledge that produces a specific value about the experience and the self in each moment of remembrance. The value attributed to the experience is drawn from the contextual factors of internally composed literary referents and externally constituted landscape markers.

The image of the protagonist, unable to speak but who stares silently at the forest due to traumatic loss, is maintained throughout the novel. This suggests a chosen silence by the individual that is paired with a transcendent listening to the nonhuman natural environment. One chapter closes with Ballantine unsuccessfully communicating with Gatlin as both men walk down a wilderness trail from the fire tower. Ballantine asks his friend what he wants to do with his life and Gatlin replies: "Stare at the sun. . . . Stare it out. Stand on this tower and stare at the sun until the sun goes . . . black" (31). Gatlin progressively ignores Ballantine's questions and then Gatlin stops and points at "something deep in the shadows among the trees" (32). The protagonist continues to search the forest for a reason or clue to Sandy's disappearance and an answer to his suffering, but chooses to remain silent, never describing what he perceives in the forest.

The novel provides a view of traumatic experience and memory through multiple memories and instances of remembering, rather than portraying trauma through a single fixed remembering that returns repeatedly. Knowledge about the traumatic experience is revealed as the narrative unfolds so that readers slowly understand events leading up to the woman's disappearance and the emotional state of the protagonist during, before, and after the event. Importantly, in the novel's portrayal of trauma, the protagonist's traumatic memories are composed of moments of pleasure between the protagonist and his beloved, as well as the painful experience of losing her. Most of the protagonist's memories are love scenes filled with playfulness and dialogues of affection, which also modifies the traditional literary trauma theory that emphasizes the "speechless horror" of the experience that caused a traumatic response. The experience that causes the protagonist's trauma is not only the actual event of her disappearance and death, but more importantly trauma is comprised of the many moments of remembering love and the pleasurable experiences with Sandy.

The formal strategies of poetic allusion, nonlinearity, and wilderness imagery function to represent trauma and the transformation of identity that produces new knowledge, not pathology, for the protagonist. Knowledge of the self and perception of the world are portrayed through the contradictory representation of wilderness that functions as a formal device to convey trauma. On the one hand, wilderness represents the inner psychological state of the protagonist. On the other hand, wilderness is an unfamiliar world that exerts a type of nonhuman agency and indifference to human suffering. In addition, the traumatic experience challenges previous formulations of the protagonist's identity, but does not suggest that the self is diseased. In contrast to claiming that trauma poses a fundamental epistemological gap, this novel encourages a different reading of the effects of traumatic experience and remembering by suggesting silence is an active choice and one that demonstrates the reformulation of subjectivity. The novel thus provides an alternative perspective regarding the acclaimed "speechlessness" or emotionally descriptive silence that often accompanies fictional descriptions of traumatic experience because silence illuminates the protagonist's curiosity of his previous formulations of subjectivity that arise in the behavior of listening to the outside world.

Ironic views on the relationship between nature and society, and the tension between the human and the wild, are conveyed through a parodic philosophical discourse based within English poetic traditions. Many poetic allusions abound, including a scene after Sandy's disappearance in which Gatlin stands on the balcony of his fire lookout tower tormented by memories of Sandy and thoughts of her dead body. Gatlin calls out to ancient heroes of classic literature in hopes that this will aid him in understanding his sorrow. He calls out to the wilderness, "like distant bugle calls, like ancient horns: *Roland! Oliver! Siegfried! Cuauhtémoc! Hamilcar! Leonidas! Joshua! Gilgamesh!*—back and back into time more remote than human memory. But thinking of her voice, the gentleness of her hands, her wild hair, her eyes in the firelight" (128). Roland refers to the Old French epic poem "Chanson de Roland" in which Roland dies in the Battle of Roncevaux, Siegfried is the heroic figure of the ancient Germanic peoples, Hamilcar is the Carthaginian general during the First Punic War, and Leonidas is the ancient Greek leader who died in the Battle of Thermopylae. Thunder accompanies Gatlin's cry for help to the ancient world of heroes who turned their sorrow into triumph. In particular, Joshua is a biblical hero who made the sun stand still while he took revenge on his enemies. Like Joshua, Gatlin wants the sun to stand still, to "stare it down" until it turns black in hopes this will assuage his sorrow. The list of heroes and their stories of suffering situate the late-modern hero's suffering within a long literary tradition that represents pain. Yet, these heroes and their suffering offer no consolation or guidance for the novel's hero. These allusions situate the novel within a cultural discourse by exploring how loss alters identity. The novel further explores themes of loss through the employment of landscape imagery which functions to convey the meaning of loss and its alteration of identity in terms not only of two lovers, but also in larger terms of the relationship between humans and the nonhuman wilderness.

The novel suggests that although traumatic experience disrupts the self, it reorders identity and the relationship between the self and external world by causing the individual to explore previous formulations of subjectivity. Nature carries multiple meanings in the novel because wilderness imagery alternates between serving as a metaphor for the protagonist's emotions and memories and as a material entity that challenges his attempts toward correspondence between the self and non-self.

The language and themes of Renaissance poetry infuse the novel's portrayal of love, loss, and the role of memory. This is particularly apparent during the flashback chapters that include lines from Thomas Wyatt's poem "They Flee From Me" (1577) that contextualize Gatlin and Sandy's love affair within European romance models. Wyatt was a significant humanist figure of the early Tudor period for his poetry and translation of humanist works like those of Petrarch. In addition, Wyatt introduced the Italian sonnet and terza rima verse form and the French rondeau into English literature (Mason 185). In both the novel and the poem, the problem of memory raises questions about how the speaker can or should relate to the absent lover, as well as how the speaker should conceptualize his own subjectivity in the wider world—as deservedly scorned lover or unjustly tormented and forsaken. For Abbey and Wyatt, the motif of the memory that interrupts functions to question the impact of the beloved's departure and the significance of suffering that the male protagonist attributes to the past. In order to appreciate the novel's reliance on Wyatt's sonnet, I quote "They Fle From Me" from the Egerton 2711 Manuscript:

They fle from me that sometyme did me seke
With naked fote stalking in my chambre.
I have sene theim gentill tame and meke,
That nowe are wyld and do not remembre
That sometyme they put theimself in daunger
To take bred at my hand; and nowe they raunge
Besely seking with a continuell chaunge.

Thancked be fortune, it hath ben othrewise
Twenty tymes better; but ons in speciall,
In thyn arraye after a pleasaunt gyse,
When her lose gowne from her shoulder did fall,
And she me caught in her armes long and small;
Therewithall swetely did my kysse,
And softely said *"dere hert, howe like you this?"*

It was no dreme: I lay brode waking.
But all is torned thorough my gentilnes,
Into a straunge fashion of forsaking;
And I have leve to go of her goodeness,
And she also to use new fangilnes.

But syns that I so kyndely ame served,
I would fain knowe what she hath deserved.[1]

The speaker recounts a memory of satisfying encounters with women,
one in particular in the second and third stanzas, but contrasts this with
his present state of bitter loneliness. The poet employs animal metaphors (probably deer) to portray a love relationship as the "game of love"
in which the lovers are represented as hunter (man) and prey (women)
(Cary 86). The end of the first stanza explains that the animals, women,
who once took bread from the speaker's hand have now become "wyld"
and uncontrollable.

Wyatt subverts typical Petrarchan oppositions between men and
women that place men in power over women by the end of the first
line, suggesting "they," the animals/women, were seeking and "stalk-

ing" *him*. The opposition between hunter and prey, man and woman, is reversed so that the speaker is, in fact, the prey. Therefore, ambiguity surrounds the power relations in love between woman and man.

In addition, the poem subverts traditional Petrarchan conventions by presenting a male lover who focuses on the physical aspects of love rather than on divinity attained through a practice of Platonic love by thinking about, not touching, the beautiful, but cruel, female beloved. Jacob Blevins convincingly shows that Wyatt deviates from Petrarchan conventions in three ways: "portraying a sexual rather than a Platonic affair; portraying the woman as having at one time pursued the now dejected lover; having the dejected lover wish emotional distress on the beloved" (280). Renaissance readers thus might view Wyatt's poem as deviant by violating expectations of the Petrarchan model of chivalrous love through the explicit focus on sexual desire. As we shall soon find, Abbey imitates Wyatt in his Petrarchan deviations, but significantly changes the representation and meaning of nature and animals. Initially in the narrative, Abbey creates nature and woman as metaphoric figures that depict the male protagonist's identity and suffering: wilderness imagery becomes a metaphor to understand Sandy, himself, and his grief. But these metaphors soon fail because nature is eventually shown as a physical entity that resists the character's solipsistic desire to articulate identity through the objectification of the external world.

The second stanza, which provides the question that Abbey's novel will ask, portrays a contradictory female figure who transforms from an image of pleasure to pain. The woman kisses the speaker and poses a rhetorical question to confirm the pleasure her kiss imparts on the man: "'dere hert, how like you this?'" The beloved's gown falls off her shoulders as she bends down to kiss the speaker, showing neither the speaker nor the lady pursuing divine virtue (Blevins 283). The question conveys several meanings based on establishing a contrast between pleasure and pain. Foremost, it invites a response from the man to comment on the pleasure he is experiencing in the "pleasant" and tender encounter. However, the question also functions to underscore the emotional pain and helplessness the speaker currently feels upon remembrance. Her question carries a hint of irony in that the memory of sexual fulfillment further creates emotional suffering for the speaker in his present solitary, "broad waking" state because the pleasure only exists in the past. This question creates an antithesis in the poem between memory and the present that Abbey's novel echoes by suggesting that the memory that interrupts is the problematic nexus of loss and grief.

The question highlights the active role of the woman and the passive role of the male speaker as he nostalgically remembers the tender exchange. Women are the protagonists in the poem, described as "free, autonomous, and somewhat ruthless creatures, pursuing the 'manly' role of choosing, courting, seducing, and abandoning their lovers" and thus creating a greater distance between courtly love conventions and Wyatt's rendering of love here, as well as between traditional ideals of male and female roles (Szalay 76). Wyatt's employment of wit, irony, and parody (also frequent techniques employed by Abbey) criticizes a medieval "Petrarchan ideal of amorous relations between the sexes" and introduces modern sexual ethics into a more complex, non-binary interpretation of love between women and men (Mason 186).

In Wyatt's poem, as in Abbey's novel, a memory haunts the speaker and conveys the degree of anguish experienced in the present when recalling the past, thus establishing a contradictory tension between past and present (line 6). The conflicting emotions of pleasure and pain leave the speaker bewildered and confused at the last line of the third stanza. He wonders what action he can take to right the wrong, or at least discontinue the suffering. The mutability of the woman, along with her inconsistency ("a straunge fashion of forsaking"), cause the speaker to request moral guidance about how to relate to her ("I would fain knowe what she hath deserved").

The sonnet also establishes an antithesis between wild and tame, pleasure and pain, between forgetting and remembering in order not only to accentuate the gap between the past and present, but to delineate the problem of the past intruding upon the present, which is the same problem Abbey presents in his novel. The wild animals that stalked the speaker with "naked fote" in his bedroom become wild and "do not remember" their sexual hunger and satiation (symbolized by the women taking bread from the speaker's hand). In contrast, the speaker remembers everything, for he cannot forget the pleasure. He reasserts that the events indeed occurred while he "lay brode waking"; it was not a dream.

Yet, like a dream, due to its haunting and evocative qualities, he remembers the woman's embrace, just as the protagonist in the novel remembers too well his lover's embrace. However, in contrast to Wyatt's poem wherein the male speaker is "forsaken" by the woman but maintains a humorous outlook on it, *Black Sun* depicts the woman's departure as a loss that is traumatic due to the unresolved memories that leave the protagonist unresponsive and tormented by the past.

Black Sun alludes to Wyatt's "They Fle From Me" on several occasions in order to situate the protagonist's experience of love and loss in relation to Wyatt's representations of male subjectivity, sexuality, and memory. The novel's most direct reference arrives in a flashback chapter that ends with the quote from line 14, in modern English without quotation marks: "*Dear heart how like you this*" (34). This question in the novel refers to the protagonist's subjectivity, like the speaker of the poem, which is marked by sexual desire and loss and located in relation to the act of remembering the beloved. The narrator describes the interaction between Gatlin and Sandy in sexual terms and employs the love game topos of hunter and prey, which is consistent with Wyatt's image of the anti-Petrarchan lover that stresses the sexual, not religious, aspects of love: "He kissed her mouth and unbuttoned her blouse" (33–34). After the kiss the narrator explains the rest of the scene: "The sun sparkled through the shaking shimmering trim translucent leaves. The warm grass surrounded them, bedded them, embraced them. An orange-black butterfly danced in the air, in the light. Monarch of the moment. . . . *Dear heart how like you this*" (34).[2] The sonnet line is left at the bottom of the page, which is also the end of the chapter, without a period or question mark. Moreover, the use of italics appears to distinguish the time frame: the entire chapter is set in the past (and written in past tense) and readers understand that the italicized last line from Wyatt is set in the present—it is Gatlin's internalized comment on remembering the scene.

The novel echoes the sonnet's motif of the memory that interrupts in order to describe the problematic relation between past and present in an effort to explore how binary paradigms of subjectivity become undone. For example, the poem's question creates an ironic tension in the novel that addresses the contradictory desire to remember and forget the past because the phrase "Dear heart how like you this" addresses the current pleasure in remembering the beloved, but also the suffering that results from the memory. Indeed, Wyatt's quote in *Black Sun* is no longer a question as found in "They Fle From Me," but now a statement of grief which further emphasizes Gatlin's despair when confronted with memories of Sandy.

The allusion acts as a deeply ironic twist to the love scene because Abbey employs Wyatt to contextualize the modern moment of love and loss within the poetic past, as well as to comment on the difference between the male speakers. In contrast to Wyatt's poem, this memory does not end with the man expressing bitterness at the woman. Abbey's male protagonist is portrayed as anguished and "lost," but not scornful of the woman (and in this regard the novel acts more conventionally Petrarchan). Thus, the novel complicates the themes of the act of remembering, the tension between past and present, and the memory that interrupts found in Wyatt's poem. Importantly, the swift transitions between memories and present reality indicate the flexibility of traumatic memories. This mutability of memory provides a view of remembering as an active process, not a fixed recall, which contradicts the traditional model that argues different types of experiences are stored in different parts of the brain. The ability of Gatlin to add to his memories in the form of internal musings on Wyatt's poem displaces the traditional model's view of trauma memory.

The "dere hert" quote in Abbey's novel situates the lovers in relation to the lovers in Wyatt's poem, as well as a poem by Chaucer. Allusions to both Wyatt and Chaucer portray Gatlin and Sandy as archetypal lovers situated in the poetic past. Dennis Kay argues that the phrase "dere hert" is a phrase employed by Chaucer in several works to suggest a liaison between two lovers: the status of the phrase is "a commonplace of intimate love dialogues" (217). Kay notes that "They Fle From Me" participates in "the *fin amor* which flourished at the court of Henry VIII, the primary inspiration for this model was Chaucer's *Troilus*" (215). Significantly, the obvious pun of the words "deer" (dear) and "hert" (deer) is employed by both Wyatt and Abbey. Wyatt's use of this phrase, according to Kay's research, is "obviously formulaic" and "morally loaded" (217–18). Consequently, Abbey's use of Wyatt's question in line 14 extends the literary tradition of "intimate love dialogues" to convey the sexual union of lovers for late-modern readers of the twentieth century. The references throughout the novel to literary historical constructions of heterosexual love and male subjectivity situated in relation to a departed female lover connect the novel to Renaissance and medieval poetic traditions, but also work to extend the humanistic dialogue on experience and knowledge by critiquing the dangers of an anthropocentric humanism that can lead to a solipsistic viewpoint.

Similar to Wyatt, Abbey relies on poetic models dating back to Petrarch and Chaucer to convey the experience of the anguished lover, the difficulty of the past intruding, and the forces that influence the process of remembering. Abbey asserts his place in the European literary tradition of romance by sharply disagreeing with its philosophical tenets and providing an alternative view of the self and world. In addition to quoting Wyatt in this love scene, the characters converse through quotes from Chaucer's poem "Merciless Beauty," further indicating Abbey's intention to contextualize the lovers within prototypical love encounters found within the romance genre. The dialogue between Gatlin and Sandy parodies Chaucer's courtly love lyric "Merciless Beauty." Once Gatlin meets Sandy in the meadow, the lovers quote lines from Chaucer's first stanza. Chaucer's poem begins:

> Youre yen two wol slee me sodeinly:
> I may the beautee of hem nat sustene,
> So woundeth it thurghout myn herte keene

Chaucer's poem is often considered an "antilyric" because although it begins with a typical "extravagant emotion of courtly love lyrics" which describes the power of the woman's eyes to "slay" the lover, the poem ends ironically with the speaker congratulating himself on his failure and good health despite the rejection. The dialogue in *Black Sun* mirrors Chaucer's mockery of love and imagery of the cruel mistress. After Gatlin "catches" Sandy in the meadow he remarks to her: "'You were expecting me'" (33). A sardonic dialogue follows with Sandy first replying: "'Yes. There.' He kissed her hair, her forehead, her darkened eyelids. . . . 'Your eyen two wol slee me sodenly. . . .' 'Chaucer wrote that.' 'You're right, lass.' 'What else do you know?' 'I may the beaute of them not sustene.' 'Slay me.' 'Yes.' 'Kiss me.' 'Yes. Shut up and I'll kiss you'"(33). After playfully invoking Chaucer, both lovers profanely express their desire in sexual terms. To a certain degree the profanity imitates Chaucer's sardonic view on love and desire. At the same time, the sexual explicitness disturbs this view by suggesting that the lovers' relationship is not based on manipulation or superficiality, but on a physical and emotional connection that Abbey further explores by returning to Wyatt's deer imagery by the end of the chapter.

The love scene in Abbey's novel below establishes a similar contrast to that found in Wyatt's poem which positions the speaker as the hunter who remembers and the female lover as prey. Like Wyatt, Abbey ironically implies by quoting Wyatt at the end of the passage that the man is hunted by the memories of Sandy, thus depicting himself as the helpless prey. The memory begins with the protagonist remembering his lover's reflection in the river as they both play in the water, then she runs away laughing:

> He pounded after her but she ran like a startled doe,
> quick with life, sprang over a log and was into the trees. . . .
> In the green gloom, she raced before him, laughing. . . .
> She collapsed suddenly on the edge of another grassy place,
> a small and sunlit opening deep in the forest. He sprawled
> upon her. . . . "You run like a rabbit. . . . First like a doe.
> Then like a rabbit." . . . [She replies] "Kiss me." . . .
> His hand moved upon her. . . . (33)

The animal imagery in this passage depicts Sandy as a deer who is chased by Gatlin. She is a "startled doe" who runs before Gatlin who "pounds" after her. Sandy is consistently figured as a deer throughout the novel and Gatlin admires "the shine of her half-wild eyes. The eyes of a doe" (68). In another sexual encounter, Gatlin says that her "vibrant body burn[s] with an animal heat" (97). Gatlin is pictured as the hunter following his prey, yet the hunter is an ambiguous figure that might be another wild animal because he is described as a "hairy old beast" who "pounds after her" rather than runs. Similar to the woman in Wyatt's poem, Sandy initiates the game of seduction. She pushes his head into the water, acting as the aggressor, and runs away. Then she "collapses" in the meadow and awaits Gatlin, ready for the sexual encounter, which again demonstrates her control of the situation. Even in the pleasure of remembering Gatlin, there remains a hint of despair because of "the green gloom" that Sandy must run through before reaching the meadow.

The novel invokes animal motifs through the exaggerated analogies between women and animals in order to comment on the comically unsettling implications of Euro-American patriarchal constructions of women, nowhere more apparent than in the character of Art Ballantine. In ways that Gatlin does not reflect Wyatt's male speaker as an anti-Petrarchan lover, Ballantine constitutes such an anti-Petrarchan male figure with his irreverence for sacred love and unrestrained sexual appetite for consuming the beloved. The novel's caricature of this hyper-masculine male in a patriarchal world works to shock the reader into reevaluating her or his own moral standards and definitions of heterosexual love, as well as the gendered roles dictated by modern society. Ballantine views the modern predicament of heterosexual love as an experience that has trapped him. He explains that love is "a social disease. A romantic, venereal, medieval disease" (28). The character expresses the lyrical thread of Wyatt's poem and animal imagery when he explains to Gatlin in a letter that his wife has left him: "They fle from me that sometyme did me seke." Abbey slightly shifts the order of Wyatt's words, but retains the poem's original meaning in order to represent Ballantine's experience of rejection. Ballantine writes: "They flee from me that once did seek me out. My delicious Darnell, she of the undulant abundant not to say redundant mammaries, has flown my coop and left me stranded. . . . master of my own dunghill and nothing much else" (76). Ballantine portrays his wife as a chicken and refers to himself as a cow and alternately as a bear (36).

The female body is described in sexually reductive terms rather than respectful spiritual ones, thus emphasizing the physical rather than reverential relations between the woman and the man. Abbey's parody in this passage demonstrates the hypocrisy in contemporary social standards that dictate gender and sexual roles for women and men wherein women are in a subjugated position. Through the parodic figure of Bal-lantine, the novel forwards a radical critique of contemporary gender conventions and sexual stereotypes. To a certain degree the character of Ballantine throws into high relief late-modern patriarchal values of the ultra-feminized and passive woman and the hypermasculinized and ac-tive man by taking these socially constructed gender roles to an extreme end. Abbey continues to utilize Wyatt's animal motif through analogies between the lost beloved and deer in the wilderness in order to show the fallacies of a Renaissance humanism that reduces nature to anthropo-morphic dimensions.

In contrast to "They Fle From Me," the deer images in *Black Sun* act as symbolic reminders of Sandy's departure and metaphorically mir-ror Gatlin's emotional states as he copes with Sandy's death. In each of the contemporary reality chapters, deer in the forest or canyon cause Gatlin to think of Sandy. The deer are dim forms on the periphery of Gatlin's vision that convey his sense of loss and ambivalent relation to the past. The first chapter shows the protagonist watching the deer and the sun rise over an alien world: "Deer are grazing at the far side of the clearing, near the foot of the fire tower—dim figures in the pearl-gray light. The dark and somber forest surrounds them all with its heavy still-ness" (13). The dark forest and dim figures correspond to the protago-nist's feelings of isolation and profound loss. Another chapter describes the nightscape as Gatlin returns to his lookout tower: "Under the old moon deer pass like phantoms through the clearing. Dead limbs of a pine grate against one another, the noise like a groan of pain, and the deer pause for a moment to listen" (136). The phantom deer that Gatlin views in the forest are figures that evoke memories of Sandy and reflect his numb, ghostlike existence. The eerie scene of tree limbs grating to produce a "groan of pain" represents the pain Gatlin feels but is unable to articulate. Both the deer and Gatlin listen to the forest, establishing a link between the two and further demonstrating Gatlin's desire for a reciprocal relationship between the external environment and his inter-nal emotional landscape. Loss is thus expressed in symbolic dimensions through landscape imagery.

Wilderness continues to function as a symbolic geography that ex-presses memory and trauma, highlighting the revisionary process of remembering. Because the protagonist does not speak about his suffering, the wilderness imagery conveys the states of shock, fear, anger, and silence induced by unexpected loss, as well as the propulsive desire to find a cure that will end the grief. Landscape imagery provides an imagistic avenue to portray an extreme emotional state.[3] In significant ways, the wilderness becomes a place that describes both the disconnected self and the self's relationship to the past. For example, the protagonist's two-week trek into the "abyss" of the canyon is an attempt to confront his feelings attached to the "horror" of Sandy's departure:

> Tortured by thirst, he crawled toward the final [water] resource
> he had prepared for days before, the disc of silver gleaming
> under the fire of the sun. Exhausted, hopeless. . . . Waking
> once again from a dream, he was struck nerveless, drawn hol-
> low by the horror of his deprivation. By the senseless sudden
> blackness of her vanishing. (146)

Abbey employs the desert environment and the protagonist's descent into the canyon to demonstrate the attempt to understand the past. The natural world provides the protagonist with the opportunity to test the boundaries of the self against an external medium to understand how the self is defined. Remembering is articulated in relation to the natural world because the physical environment provides a referent for identity that delineates what is human versus not human. In this fashion, the desert wilderness acts as a signpost between perceptions of the self and external world, and between the past and contemporary present.

The protagonist remains uncertain of the referential points between the self and natural world and appears even less clear about the purpose of his life after this foray into the wild. As he walks farther in the canyon, the demarcations between self and non-self, between the present experience of the natural world and the past, seem to overlap and evaporate to the extent that the protagonist cannot rely upon previous formulations of self situated in relation to a fixed nonhuman world. As the protagonist descends a thousand feet to the canyon floor near the Colorado River, he encounters "dangerous" animals and temperatures that exceed 126 degrees:

> There were no trees, not even the scrubbiest of junipers,
> nothing but the knee-high brush, the dusty desert, the pale
> glaring stone which made his squinting eyes burn and
> ache. . . . But no trace of what he was searching for. . . .
> What did he really expect to find? . . . A broken body draped
> on rock, a thin cry for help? (143)

Questioning his motives for the search reveals that looking for Sandy is just as much about confronting his own feelings about her disappearance as it is about locating a definitive answer to her whereabouts. However, the protagonist's search for Sandy does not provide the cure he seeks. The desert still reminds him of her absence and makes evident his disconnection from nature.

The novel's representation of nature as both a reflection of the protagonist's psychological states and as an unfamiliar world complicates the Renaissance humanist myths of romance and subjectivity situated in terms of the relation between the human and the wild. Nature reminds the protagonist of loss, but the desert, the forest, and the animals within these ecosystems also exist as entities with their own forms of agency. Wilderness functions beyond symbolic terms because nature exists as an alternate nonhuman world that rebukes the protagonist's attempt to assimilate it into his consciousness as merely a metaphor. In the canyon, the protagonist searches for his beloved and calls out for a response, but is only confronted with the indifferent gaze of animals:

> Across the chasm of time and an inconsolable loss he sees the
> soft glow of her hair, her timid smile. "Sandy?" The deer lift
> their heads at the sound of his voice, stare up at him not in
> surprise, not in fear, but with a calm, unruffled, almost com-
> placent consideration, as at a noise familiar, harmless, but
> infrequent. (79)

The sense of loss is exacerbated by the indifferent stare of the external world. The wilderness, in the form of deer, moves beyond metaphoric reference because it is presented as unaffected by human society and emotional suffering. The ecological ethos here suggests that humans are not the center of meaning in the world and fall short of providing a referential marker for value in the larger universe.

Throughout the narrative the wilderness acts as a material entity that resists Gatlin's attempt to metaphorize it. Although the woman is compared to the enigmatic quality of deer and their desires, ultimately the deer are nonhuman animals, unconcerned with human affairs. Nature maintains agency in the sense that the protagonist must come to terms with the fact that the wilderness is simply the wilderness, mostly indifferent to him. Before Gatlin returns to the plateau, he sees vultures crowding over a carcass that he first thinks is Sandy's body:

> Tears, of which he was unaware, streamed through the
> stubble of beard on his face. He groaned, gasped for breath,
> clawing at the brush and loose stones as he struggled down
> the final incline and reached the crest. He rushed down, they
> [vultures] raised their dripping beaks, vomited, scattered, beat-
> ing the air with long and heavy wings. . . . Halfway down the
> slop Gatlin stopped. The quarry was only a deer, a small doe
> battered and partly dismembered by a long fall from the cliff
> above. . . . He paused to rest, turning his back on the glare,
> and gazed with weary, aching, blood-flecked eyes at the world
> of the canyon. He was alone in one of the loneliest places
> on earth. . . . Alone. Was he alone? "Sandy!" he howled. And
> waited for an answer. (149)

The deer are mutable figures in this passage that multiply represent Sandy, Gatlin's relation to the past, and nonhuman species. At first the deer symbolize Gatlin's fear of the probability of Sandy's death, but then they are viewed as part of a nonhuman ecological system. The suffering and sorrow that Gatlin experiences as he nears what he imagines to be Sandy's body shows the proximity of traumatic memory to his current identity. The traumatized protagonist rushes to the "scene" of the painful past, coming face to face with the figure that has represented Sandy for him throughout their love affair and whose "dim figure" in the forest recalls Sandy's absence. He struggles down the "final incline" to face the fact of her death, but is turned away with the realization that it is "only a deer." He still cannot incorporate Sandy's death, as he shouts out her name and waits for an answer. When he cries her name wondering if he is alone and waiting for something or someone to speak back, he is confronted with no reassurances of belonging in the world, only a strong sense of disconnection. In the depth of the protagonist's emotional pain, he is confronted with an ecological scene that rebukes his suffering: a primal interaction between predator and prey that disrupts his initial perspective on his identity and the purpose of his desert journey, which was to find redemption or closure in the wilderness or a sense of reciprocity. The protagonist is only left "waiting" with no answers and no healing.

The protagonist perceives the canyon as an "abyss" of shadows and "deeper darkness" to the extent that both the desert and loss remain partially incomprehensible. This reinforces a view of the wild as a strange physical sphere of action and instills the need to listen to this world in order to potentially fully perceive it. The narrative points out that the myth of humans' ability to fully know nature through an imagined unmediated interaction and connection between the human and the wild is a persistent desire in the text that is consistently constructed only to be undercut. At one stage during his search, Gatlin encounters a rattlesnake: "He crouches low and peers directly into the eyes of the snake. 'Cousin,' he cries, 'What have you done with her?' The bleak and dusty eyes stare back at him, the thin black tongue slips in and out as the snake attempts to sense the nature of this unknown danger" (91). He seeks some response from the external world as to her whereabouts and to the meaning of her death, but he finds no meaning or reassurance from the wilderness surrounding him.

Similar to the above passage, other chapters in the novel portray animals less as a representation of the protagonist's psychological states and more as figures of a mysterious antihuman wilderness. In the following scene the protagonist at first imagines that Sandy calls his name, reinforcing the point that he has not accepted her death, but is confronted only with deer staring at him:

> Returning to the cabin, buckling his belt, he is halted by a soft
> voice . . . *Will* . . . calling his name. . . . He stops, looks back

and around, searches the depths of the forest. But there is
nothing. He sees only what is there, the living and dying trees,
the flowers of red and purple penstemon crowding the trunk
of a fallen pine, the dim form farther back of a single yearling
doe, its head up and alert, facing him. Listening. . . . He
listens. (35–36)

Although Gatlin notices "there is nothing" in the forest, this recognition
is followed by a factual sentence that describes details of the forest, trees,
color, species of flowers, and a deer. The voice calling out to him is the
memory of his beloved and the memory of her departure and death.

The contradiction between seeing "nothing" and identifying the environment as a naturalist might observe it suggests that the protagonist
sees the wilderness as an entity without a human presence as well as a
concrete boundary that delineates what is memory and what is actual
perception. This sentence with its emphasis on "only" evokes the present moment and indicates the limitations of completely perceiving the
world. But this line between memory and reality often collapses during
mourning, especially when Gatlin treks into the canyon. Gatlin does not
find Sandy, and thus sees "nothing." The imagined voice vanishes as
quickly as the memory when he labels the natural world by what can be
seen. The passage ends with two words, "He listens," in order to highlight the grief and anticipation of Sandy's return. Just as the earlier example shows the deer listening to the eerie rub of tree limbs, Gatlin listens
along with the deer. The protagonist remains suspended in an anticipa-
tory moment for the event that never happens: the return of his beloved.

The protagonist's listening and silence continue throughout the
novel. He stares into a forest that becomes increasingly foreign and
"strange" as he searches for evidence of Sandy. The strangeness of the
wild resists the protagonist's attempts to find answers to Sandy's disappearance or his own suffering. Nature therefore fails to provide a place
of healing or regeneration. In the first chapter, Gatlin is drawn to the
abyss of the canyon, the rupture in the plateau that is "vast" and "fath-
omless," similar to his memories of Sandy that threaten to consume
him (15).

However, even after his journey into the canyon and confrontation of

the memories that haunt him, both the wild and the past remain beyond elucidation. The canyon remains "something strange, a great cleft dividing the plateau from end to end, an abyss where the pale limestone walls of the rim fall off into a haze of shadows, and the shadows down into a deeper darkness" (15). The last chapter ends with Gatlin staring "out the window, into the forest," unresponsive to questions from Ballantine (157). This silence is paired with a deep listening to the wild in an effort to show the alternating intimacy and disconnection that marks the protagonist's relationship to both the past and the external environment. Silence functions as a rhetorical strategy to convey the protagonist's difficulty in coming to terms with the traumatic experience.

Similar to *Monkey Bridge* and *Ceremony*, silence in *Black Sun* conveys a variety of individual and cultural values that include connotations of internal imbalance as well as a refusal to accept the world as previously formulated. In all three novels, nature is viewed by the traumatized protagonist as a multifaceted arena of action and emotion that holds a spectrum of value linked to cultural beliefs. In *Black Sun* these cultural beliefs are linked to European themes of love and loss, in Cao's novel the beliefs of karma and the betel nut myth shape the remembrance of suffering, and in Silko's novel the hybrid indigenous storytelling of battles between good and evil influences how the protagonist relates to his feelings and the past.

In Abbey's novel as well as Silko's novel, remembering is a reconstruction that contains physicality within the process: Gatlin must walk into the canyon to confront his thoughts and Tayo must walk through the hoops of the sandpainting ceremony and look onto the desert lands as he recovers his internal coherence. These characters are not trying to find a fossilized moment in the past. The ceremonial actions that occur in direct relation to nature allow the characters to interact with their own feelings and comprehend their emotions. In Cao's novel, Thanh is unable to physically inhabit a landscape or interact with a natural environment in which a ceremonial or ritualistic action could take place. Rather, Thanh's ceremonial action is found in writing a story to her daughter in which she expresses a karmic belief of a negative destiny that has befallen her.

Abbey's novel embodies the disorientation and suffering caused by trauma through the rhetorical use of silence and achronological plot. The disruption caused by trauma, however, does not "shatter" the protagonist because he still maintains agency as one who willfully makes choices about the course of his life after the traumatic event. The experience throws the protagonist into an emotional suffering and type of isolation that, paradoxically, cause him to reevaluate previous assumptions of self and relation to the world. The protagonist wants to stare at the sun until it turns black due to the intensity of his grief. Yet, perhaps more than a personal death wish, this is a plea to stop time and remembering, as well as slow the changing perceptions of self and world caused by trauma. In this regard, wilderness imagery functions to demonstrate that one response to traumatic experience is a type of silence that involves a listening to the outside world. Silence is different than "disarticulation" because the novel makes clear that the experience and its remembrance may generate a verbal silence in the protagonist, but not an emotional muteness. The novel therefore suggests that one response to a traumatic experience is a type of silence that is rendered as a profound listening to and awareness of the natural world.

In addition, the novel imagines the location of traumatic experience and remembering in terms of the reformulation of subjectivity. The reorientation of consciousness indicates that one's perception of the world is revisionary through a remembering process that accords a range of values gathered from the physical environment and literary traditions. The contextual factor of the wilderness draws the reformulation of consciousness into a larger discussion regarding the value of pain in society. Although there is not a healing trajectory in the novel as is found in *Ceremony,* and contact with the wilderness does not exert a curative power, the protagonist's own realization of finding "no remedy" may work as an acknowledgment of the changed self. In the canyon, Gatlin thinks: "Somewhere down in there [the underworld] she may still be alive, waiting for you. . . . No. There is no remedy. The river sings, a mad chaotic babble of many voices" (91). The radical reorientation of the self is based primarily in relation to the natural environment, thereby producing a rhetoric of identity located within a larger ecological sphere of action. To this end, nature harvests a different economy of emotion than society that works toward defining the self.

CHAPTER FIVE

Neocolonialism and Polluted Places
in Robert Barclay's *Melal*

Robert Barclay's *Melal: A Novel of the Pacific* (2002) explores the traumatic displacement and dispossession of land and community as the result of colonial and imperial pursuits. The historical novel draws a portrait of a neocolonized people in the 1980s Marshall Islands who are living with the consequences of an American colonial government that dropped nuclear "test" bombs, displaced thousands of Marshallese, and caused major health problems from radiological waste. The postnuclear setting and the inability to inhabit one's homeland create an ironic tension that highlights the paradoxes of the modern human condition.

The Marshallese protagonists of the novel are the Keju family. Rujen, the father, and his older son, Jebro, live in a period in 1981 when their government has a form of sovereignty and, in fact, the nation is close to independence (historically this occurs in 1986). The Marshallese family live on Ebeye Island, which has limited fresh water, poor sanitation, and frequent energy outages, located only three miles from the wealthy, industrialized, American-only island of Kwajalein with a U.S military base. The socioeconomic oppression of the colonized is paired with another form of environmental oppression due to the fact that Marshallese protagonists are unable to return to their radioactive rural atolls that were their homelands for generations. In addition, the death of Jebro's mother is caused by the U.S. military atomic bomb tests on nearby islands. The inability to return to generationally inhabited atolls because of the contamination of the land and sea, coupled with the unjust socioeconomic daily conditions, create the major tensions in the novel for the protagonists. This conflict is expressed in relation to a Pacific landscape and seascape, otherwise referred to as the terramarine environment, which is a place that not only contains the economic, cultural, ecological, and emotional components of life for the father and son, but also influences their sense of self and relationship to society.

Functioning within a neocolonial framework, *Melal* gestures toward a recovery of land, a complex relationship to a traumatic past, and an ideological resistance to Western capitalism and nuclear weaponry as a way to define a Marshallese identity. However, the government and people of the Marshall Islands, even when political independence seems near at hand in the novel, will remain economically colonized, controlled, and crippled by a larger power—the United States. I use the term "neocolonialism" to refer to the merging of colonialism and imperialism (also called postcolonialism) wherein the colonial era entails "direct military or settler occupation" and imperialism is an "economic or cultural system of structural inequality" (Brennan 6). Timothy Brennan, establishing early theories on empire, writes: "The United States continues to invade other countries, but the invasion is not now supposed to be an invasion: rather, the nation extends its shadow, *becomes* the elsewhere, decenters itself" (6). In the novel's time frame, the Marshall Islands exist in a neocolonial situation with the U.S. government extending its power through economic controls over the Marshallese community.

The Marshallese protagonists maintain no legal rights to reclaim land taken by the U.S. military in the colonial era, and the atomic refuse of the colonial era still exerts its grasp on the health of the population. Nevertheless, the protagonists resent and resist a foreign nation that utilizes nature as a machine-like resource to maintain global dominance through the production and use of nuclear bombs and ballistic missiles. The protagonists see nature as a living organism that contains individual and collective memories. Interactions with the Pacific seascape are valued as a place that sustains life. Individual identity is therefore not defined as a resistance to a colonial or imperial power, or necessarily in relation to a collective traumatic historical past. Rather, Marshallese identity is reconceived by survival in the face of deadly contaminants and a relationship to a postnuclear landscape within a society that economically depends upon the very nation that produces the toxic pollution—the United States of America.

The novel follows the lives of the Keju family who live on Ebeye Island during a single day in 1981. On the morning of this day, two adolescent brothers, Jebro and Nuke, take a fishing trip to Tar-Woj Island and experience a boating disaster. The boys' father, Rujen, who works at the United States missile-range facility on Kwajalein Island in the sewage division, experiences his own emotional crisis at work that continues when he attends a church service. Rujen is the traumatized protagonist who never directly addresses the death of his wife caused by radiation exposure. However, he eventually does challenge the colonial power structure that caused her death and created a society in which he and his family endure discrimination.

The novel also follows the supranatural action of a tragic mythic narrative that occurs between gods and spirits: Noniep, the sorcerer-healer, Wullep, the demon, and Etao, a trickster who helps Noniep. These characters enact a mythology of indigenous inhabitation of the islands and the meeting of ancient and modern cultures on the nuclear waste site that the Marshallese protagonists call home. The actions of the gods and spirits exemplify the human struggle of the Keju family as well as the natural world's fight for survival. In this way, the ecological and indigenous myth-rituals inform the depiction of loss that is inextricably tied to specific places, which further highlights the function of myths as a contextual factor of trauma in fiction.

The mythological reality of the supranatural characters and plot is presented as a ritualistic battle between good and evil that takes place in the sky and sea, in the atemporal heavens and the finite, quotidian life of human beings on and around the islands. Noniep's prologue initiates the myth ritual of the novel in the opening pages when he is seen on the atoll of Tar-Woj where he views the fight between demons and dwarfs-sorcerers who are healers like himself. He watches these forces in battle on Ebeye: "Noniep dreams of demons he has fought and destroyed. . . . He dreams of a plan, a hope, a small and unrealistic chance of stopping what looms like a monstrous wave risen to precarious height" (14). The mythic action connects to the human social performance of the Keju brothers' struggle to find their ancestral homeland and cope with their geographic and socioeconomic displacement. Action and myth, according to Alexander, Giesen, and Mast, provide the audience access to a collective authentic reality that stands beyond reason or social structure and as such serves as a grounding element of a community (6). Although Alexander tends toward an essentialist notion of place, my discussion presses for the relational and ever changing value of place. Geographic and mythical spaces are organized into places in different ways and for diverse purposes by each character in the novel.

In emphasizing the transformation of space into place or the varying value attached to certain places, I underscore the fluidity of place in the sense of the shifting meaning linked to a place. The particular place of a traumatic event, such as the river in Cao's novel where the character Thanh is hit with napalm, or the Pacific atolls of previous inhabitation and current nuclear weapon experiments in Barclay's novel, as well as the place of the remembrance of trauma, such as the desert canyon where Abbey's protagonist attempts to find the missing woman, conveys a variety of values for the traumatized protagonist and the narrative as a whole. However, these values attached to a place are not permanent.

The meaning of a place, whether in a natural or an urban environment, changes and comes into focus or refocus within different contextual paradigms of knowledge and experience. George Handley emphasizes the unfixed and evolving creation of place when he says that one "recreates [a] sense of place always in the present" (10). This view challenges the argument by some scholars who forward a transhistorical trauma theory to assert an essentialist (and nationalistic) concept of place insofar that the value of a place is fixed and unchanging. From this perspective, place is imagined in such a way as to harbor "ghosts" of the past: a landscape stands as an unwavering symbol of past traumas and the land represents the present-day victim status of peoples associated with that landscape, thus working to become consolidated into a national victim-based identity. Karen Till argues that national identity is codified through social memory fixed to a place because a place inherently mummifies social memory and hence national identity: "Places haunted by past structures of meaning may also evoke, confront, or encrypt transgenerational phantoms."[1] In Maria Tumarkin's *Traumascapes,* she carries forth the traditional trauma model to assert

that "for places across the world marked by traumatic legacies of violence, suffering, and loss, the past is never quite over" (12). Transhistorical trauma theory merges with place theory in the author's attempt
to show that once a place is "transformed physically and psychically by
suffering," the place or traumascape becomes "part of a scar tissue that
now stretches across the world" (13).

Place in Barclay's novel is imagined through different connections
and inhabitations by a range of diverse people. Each person or group
creates significant meaning and mythic symbolism that arises from
myriad sources and factors. Place, like the concept of nation, is imagined. Benedict Anderson argues that nation "is an imagined political
community—and imagined as both inherently limited and sovereign"
(9). Similar to the nation, place comes into being as an imagining, an
act of remembering, but an act that is tied to one's experience in a physical environment. The concept of place does not suggest a fixed rhetorical construct. In each novel, place as a concept, physical entity, and
functional part of the plot is depicted in many ways, at times contradic-
torily and from multiple points of views, which challenges the view by
scholars such as Till or Tumarkin who appear to advocate an essentialist
notion of place to support a claim for a tranhistorical victimized national
identity.

The setting of the novel shows a Marshallese culture on the cusp of
becoming an independent nation. In this way the novel expresses both
colonial and postcolonial thematic tendencies due to the examination of
the effects of domination by the United States that include unbalanced
neoliberal trade patterns between the colony and empire, and nuclear
waste and contamination. The term "empire" refers to a centrally controlled powerful nation ruled by an oligarchy that dominates a group
of less powerful states and peoples.[2] The discursive framework of the
novel explores the effects of colonization and the multilayered and ubiq-
uitous forms of domination experienced by the Marshallese population
in a neoimperial era. This depiction highlights a view of U.S. imperialism articulated by Donald Pease as "a complex and interdependent relationship with hegemonic as well as counterhegemonic modalities of
coercion and resistance" (23). In particular, the traumatic experiences of
displacement, relocation, death of family members, and illness from the

atomic bombs in the past, as well as the continuing disease and health consequences from radioactive and ballistic waste in the present, combine to produce an environment of physical and emotional imprisonment. There is a physical disease produced from the radioactive waste of the bombs and an emotional consequence of displacement from homelands, but these experiences are not shown to produce a psychic disease or transhistorical trauma. The death of Rujen's wife was a traumatic experience for him as well as his children and other family members. For the elder son, Jebro, the isolation from his ancestral homelands creates a profound distress. Importantly, the traumatic events of the past interact with the protagonists in the form of memories and the actions of supranatural characters.

Barclay's novel addresses the problems of self-determination and civic equality for colonized peoples under a colonial regime, but pays special attention to the emotional responses caused by the nuclear "test" bombing. Rujen as the traumatized protagonist references the historical events of the colonization of the Marshall Islands and the nuclear bombing on these Asian Pacific islands by the United States. The figure of the traumatized protagonist in the novel suggests that an individual's response to a traumatic experience changes over time and shows that characters respond differently to the same event. For example, Rujen is directly affected by the nuclear bombs because this radiation exposure killed his wife and displaced his family and community. Yet, he did not respond in the same way his father did, even though he also experienced the bombs. Extreme events in the novel that large groups of people experienced elicit particular emotional responses in specific ways for each character who reacts to the event and to the memories of the event in her or his own fashion.

The title of the novel, *Melal,* is derived from an archaic Marshallese word that means a playground of demons and a place uninhabitable by people. For Barclay, the word specifically refers to the Kwajalein, Ebeye, and Tar-Woj islands in the Kwajalein Atoll. This is the site of sixty-seven nuclear weapons tested by the United States military between 1946 and 1958, including thermonuclear devices and the government's first hydrogen bomb. The historical background of the novel is the 1954 U.S. hydrogen bomb test on Bikini Atoll (code name Castle Bravo) that carried dangerous radiological fallout 150 miles from the site to many inhabited islands, including Rongelap Atoll, which was not evacuated.[3]

Rongelap Atoll plays an important role in the novel, for it is the homeland for the characters' relatives. The dropping of this hydrogen bomb is considered one of the worst radiological accidents by the United States government. Due to a laboratory error, coupled with the director's disregard for increased wind patterns, the bomb yielded fifteen megatons, rather than the expected four megatons, creating a fireball three miles across and a mushroom cloud that reached 47,000 feet in the first minute, then climbed to 130,000 feet in the next ten minutes.[4] To place this into perspective, the bomb was 1,000 times more powerful than the atomic bomb that was dropped on Hiroshima.[5]

People on Rongelap and other atolls were exposed to near-fatal levels of radiation but were only evacuated *after* the bomb was dropped. Nearly 20,000 people were moved off the islands within a few days of the bomb to Kwajalein and medically treated, but up to twenty years later the inhabitants on nearby islands showed high rates of thyroid tumors, leukemia, and birth defects.[6] The people exposed to radiation were medically observed and tracked long after the event without their knowledge or consent in a U.S. government program that recorded the effects of radiation on the human body.[7] Many of those evacuated were moved back to Rongelap Island after being told it was safe three years later, even though government documents now reveal evidence that the United States Brookhaven Laboratory sent islanders back to Rongelap to study the effects of radiation on humans.[8] The Marshallese were relocated multiple times from island to island, and most were never able to return to their homes due to the radioactive pollution. Rongelapians were evacuated in 1985 due to high rates of thyroid tumors and other health problems linked to radioactive contamination. In addition, today there are extremely high rates of tuberculosis on Ebeye due to the tremendous overcrowding and poor sanitation where 12,000 people, the majority of the Marshallese, are forced to live on an eighty-acre island, resulting in one of the most densely populated places in the world.[9]

Kwajalein Atoll of the Marshall Islands, the locus of action in Barclay's novel, is one of the largest atolls on the planet. It is situated within the Ralik chain of islands, located between Hawaii and Papua New Guinea. Many of the islands were devastated when American forces invaded and took over the area from the Japanese occupation during World War II. After the war, the United States occupied the islands and entered into an agreement in 1947 with the United Nations Security Council to administer and control Micronesia, including the Marshall Islands, as a trust territory. The area was under foreign domination for a span of 100 years: it went from being a colony of Germany in 1885, to a territory of Japan during World War II, and then a colony of America from 1947 to 1986.

When the nuclear testing program came to an end in the area, the islands became an essential component in America's "Star Wars" strategic defense program. In 1965, the American military again relocated the people on most of Kwajalein's islands, so that a large area of the lagoon and some of the islands could be used as target sites for ballistic missile deployment. The Marshall Islands attained a form of independence in 1986 from United States rule and trusteeship. However, a recently amended and approved compact between the U.S. and Marshallese governments allows the United States government continued use of the lagoon and its ninety islands as a military test range until the year 2086.[10] Under the compact, the "United States has full authority and responsibility for security and defense of the Marshall Islands, and the Government of the Marshall Islands is obligated to refrain from taking actions that would be incompatible with these security and defense responsibilities" (U.S. Department of State 1). Today, the Marshallese technically have a form of sovereignty, but the restraints placed upon their political and economic systems make the Republic of the Marshall Islands a de facto U.S. colony that operates under a neocolonial socioeconomic structure.

Barclay's novel historically reflects the differences between the lives of Americans and Marshallese in the region during the 1980s, wherein Americans are granted full citizen rights and socioeconomic benefits on Kwajalein Island, while the Marshallese are denied these same benefits, have a curfew on Kwajalein, and live on Ebeye. Most Marshallese are forced to live on the overcrowded island of Ebeye but take the ferry to travel a short distance in order to work for the U.S. government on Kwajalein where social and economic segregation is enforced, much like in the American South until the late 1960s.

The narrative highlights the extreme difference between the wealth of the Americans living on Kwajalein and the poverty and sickness of Marshallese living only three miles away on Ebeye in order to show the reduced possibility of future freedoms for children, exemplified by brothers Jebro and Nuke. In the first chapter Jebro sees a sign outside an American restaurant on Kwajalein that reads: NO MARSHALLESE ALLOWED ON THESE PREMISES. ANYBODY CAUGHT WILL FACE IMPRISONMENT AND WILL BE RUINED (8). This sign warns of the limited access to equal civic rights as well as the limited ability to move and act freely on their own land.

The Keju family and Marshallese community face the socioeconomic domination of the United States also through the effects of radiological contamination from the Castle Bravo bomb in 1954, resulting in the recurring displacement from homelands. Rujen's father experienced the bomb and displacement, as did his wife, Iia, who lived on Rongelap and was exposed to radiation when she saw the fireball and mushroom cloud of the bomb. Iia explained her experience of the Castle Bravo bomb when she was a girl living on Rongelap:

> By that night people began to vomit. Their skin and their eyes
> and their mouths became inflamed, burning hot . . . after
> about ten days the hair on their heads and their body hair was
> falling away, their burned skin was peeling off in patches,
> their fingernails were becoming discolored and falling off,
> their fingers bleeding. (81)

The mother eventually died from the radiological exposure several years after Jebro and Nuke were born. After giving birth to Jebro, she sees that he has been born with a "deformity," an extra finger on his left hand. The effects of the bomb linger to the present time of the novel, not merely in radiation-related health problems, but due to the fact that the Marshallese characters can never return to their home islands or atolls.

The experience of nuclear radiation, long-lasting health problems, and massive geocultural displacement create loss and anger for both

Jebro and his father. Their resentment toward the occupying government and culture is a result of a collection of experiences that revolve
around the dispossession of homelands (rural atolls), family members'
deaths from forced radiological exposure, and socioeconomic inequality. The postnuclear sites of the rural atolls are the native homelands to
most Marshallese living on Ebeye, but are not occupied due to contamination and the ongoing use of ballistic missiles. Jebro's matrilineal clan
inhabited Mālu for generations, but it remains uninhabitable:

> Mālu was poisoned by radioactive fallout from the sixty-six
> atomic and hydrogen thermo-nuclear bombs detonated nearby
> at Bikini and Enewetak. Jebro might live and die without ever
> setting foot on his rightful land at Mālu, but knowing that it
> was there, that he belonged to it and it to him, gave his life
> profound meaning and position. (80)

Being unable to live or even visit his matrilineal homeland and the land
of his parents and grandparents makes Jebro feel "cheated," but the
knowledge that these places still exist provides comfort and a sense of
identity rooted in family relations and culture (260). This is why Jebro
sails to Tar-Woj, the place of his patrilineal clan, to visit his grandfa-
ther's grave and to feel a connection to his family, even though he is
forbidden by U.S. law due to possible contamination and ballistic missiles (90).

The abandoned rural atolls are remembered by the protagonists as
a contradictory source of a geoculturally based identity: the atolls are
a source of dangerous contamination and place of trauma, as well as a
source of ancestral knowledge that influences a Marshallese identity. In
particular, the rural atolls are a location more imagined than inhabited
by the protagonists, thus giving rise to late-modern narratives of identity and home en absentia. Home is a place geographically situated and
proximally close, yet uninhabitable, thereby creating perceptions of the
self and world that feel at times discordant. However, Barclay does not
draw out a picture of a victimized cultural identity, but rather suggests
a resilient identity that resists oppression as a form of survival in a so-
ciopolitically hostile environment. The sense of loss is a facet of life for

each of the three members in the Keju family and this loss is only one aspect, not the defining feature.

The atolls, lagoons, waterways, coastlines, and ocean margins are places that influence Jebro's identity and sense of belonging to a family, community, and ecologic environment. Yet, the radioactively wasted rural atolls throw into doubt the protagonist's hope for an independent and sustainable future. The value of a place for Jebro is gained by a compilation of factors that include the physical location of inhabited and uninhabited atolls and the symbolic meanings and representations attached to these places. Lang suggests that "deciphering the meaning of place requires looking at the physical dimensions as well as interpreting its symbolic meaning" (83). The island Tar-Woj is a specific place that is not only a physical location that excites memories and feelings for Jebro, but also functions symbolically to express Jebro's perception of the world from the vantage point of being accepted and welcomed in this world. David Gegeo argues that identity is marked not only by occupation of a particular physical space, but also by the action of memory and imagination that occurs in a cognitive cultural "place."[11]

The novel shows that Jebro's identity is not defined only by the displacement caused by the Castle Bravo bomb and fallout, a symbol of foreign oppression by the U.S. empire. Rather, Jebro's sense of self is influenced most strongly by a claim of belonging to a particular terramarine place on rural islands. Tar-Woj Atoll and Rongelap Atoll near the island of Mālu, where the boys set sail at the start of the novel, are the sites of nuclear devastation: this landscape is a reminder of displacement and loss, yet also a site that acts as a source of social and political freedom. It is a starting point for an articulation of identity defined beyond the American military-industrial complex (260).

As such a place of possibility, Tar-Woj allows the brothers to reconsider and re-create new narratives of the self, family, and the relation to both their homelands and to the foreign U.S. domination. While sitting on the shore of Tar-Woj, Jebro tells his younger brother: "Marshallese can never live like in the past. . . . I'm a fisherman. . . . I'll take that Kwajalein job and do the Americans' dirty work, but I won't be some worker with a fishing hobby. I'll be a fisherman whose hobby is a job making money. I have my own life, not one the Americans give me. To them I am just a slave, nobody" (130). This local or indigenous perspective of identity is what Susan Najita calls "indigenous efforts toward social re-distribution in the forms of self-determination and sovereignty" in the face of the "political and economic legacy of colonialism" (12). The older brother understands that economic dependence on a foreign power is necessary for survival, but believes that economic dependence will be worked out on his own terms, not the government's. Fishing accords with an indigenous worldview that functions largely outside the global economic market, thereby supporting an existence and consciousness that are not directly controlled by foreign commerce.

This passage underscores the perspective in the novel that a sense of an individual self is not tied necessarily to a traumatic experience in the past, a nation, or a national consciousness constructed in opposition to an imperial nation. This emphasizes the point made by George Hand-ley that "both one's cultural identity and one's sense of place are not to be pursued with a singular perspective" (9). Furthermore, ecological disaster and social dislocation caused by the machinations of foreign dominance and supranatural events propel the protagonists to reposi-tion themselves in relation to the natural world and local Marshallese communities and families:

> Jebro's greatest claim to land was at Rongelap, on the island of
> Mālu, where his mother and her clan, *ripako ran* (shark clan),
> once had lived. . . . Jebro had known of his rights at Mālu for
> as long as he could remember, as most Marshallese children,
> no matter where they were located, relocated, exiled, or re-
> settled, were taught very early their *jowi*, the designation name
> of their *bwij*, their clan, and taught from this what lands were
> theirs to call home. (78–79)

The sense of belonging to a place links Jebro to the atolls and sea, ma-jor referents for identity in the narrative. His clan name of shark refer-ences the power to assert his agency and rights and the potential danger or threat to the empire that the boy contains with this knowledge. The protagonist perceives his home and freedom as limited to uninhabitable atolls. Yet, even though he feels displaced, the awareness of his natural (civic) rights under any government enables him to sustain a resistance of consciousness to the oppressive foreign power.[12]

The rural atolls carry a personal value and cultural meaning for Jebro, but the value of these places is also imagined in terms of a U.S.-controlled global marketplace of economic, political, and military power. In this regard, Jebro and Nuke's fishing trip to Tar-Woj shows a desire to connect to the past and their ancestry, even though the boys are aware that their future survival seems inevitably bound to the modern, industrial power of the United States government. Muir and Weissman argue that construction of a place is used to "delineate, comment on, and transform the social order of the city" (82). John Agnew and James Duncan argue that place "serves not only as an indicator but as a source of social and political order. . . . [and] as a constantly re-energized repository of socially and politically relevant traditions and identity which serves to mediate between the everyday lives of individuals . . . and the national and supranational institutions which constrain and enable those lives" (7). The repository of values found in Tar-Woj is not necessarily directional or oppositional between self and state or colonized and colonizer, but rather a mix of multiple input sources from individuals, nations, and myths.

Although the terramarine environment of the islands is the site of empowered ancestral identity, it is also the source of continued socioeconomic oppression due to the seizure of land and the censure of civic rights by the U.S. military, which creates a conflicted relationship with the foreign power. The contradictory relationship between the Marshallese and American governments and peoples is presented within an imperial paradigm tied to a place that evokes but moves beyond the colonial relationship between colonizer and colonized:

> Jebro saw that Ebeye was land made ugly, but for many Marshallese it was also New York, Tokyo, Hong Kong, Manila, the closest a Marshallese might ever get to experiencing the life such places offered. Ebeye had television and a movie house— rural atolls did not. Ebeye had new and exotic foods, electricity, beer, discos, drugs, cars and trucks, and missiles flying overhead, and it held the possibility of working for good money on

Kwajalein, working for America, the most powerful nation on Earth. Even Jebro, however much he recognized Ebeye's obscenity, could not reject what it offered him. Ebeye, for Jebro, was like a shark on whose nose he rode to avoid its teeth. (79).

The shark imagery of riding the nose of the beast to avoid its bite and certain ensuing death points toward the traps of imperialism, and the benefits of utilizing the energy of the ferocious animal to survive. The shark metaphor corresponds to Jebro's clan name, ripako, to suggest the doubled or bicultural life and the pull of competing worldviews.

Moreover, the turn-of-the-century discourse that arises in the novel broadens the master-slave relationship between empire and colony. This reflects a perspective articulated by Homi Bhabha and Ania Loomba regarding a colonial discourse that attempts to fix identities between master and slave but instead works to destabilize and hybridize these very categories.[13] In this new model of dominance and loss in Barclay's novel, one's resistance to oppression is not primarily predicated upon land retrieval, since the decimated lands and polluted sea are not viable home places. In other words, the "occupied" territory in the novel as a geopolitical place moves beyond a colonial paradigm because the terramarine environment, rather than necessarily physically or even ideologically occupied, is contaminated and toxic, thus likely never a safe spot to dwell or reclaim. To a certain degree, the text depicts the local and global interdependencies at work in a neocolonial Pacific region that also exists as a site of resistance for neocolonized peoples. Rob Wilson and Arif Dirlik argue that the Asia-Pacific is a region *and* a discourse because it is "a conjunction of local culture and global economy spreading across this region both as a subcontracted networking and as micropolitical identity" which creates a "space of cultural production" and "location of postmodern resistances" (2).[14]

The collected possibilities listed in the novel's passage above show some of the benefits of an American culture based on the unequal divide created between a subsistence-fishing livelihood versus an industrial, urban existence. However, Jebro still gravitates toward the rural atolls, the sea, and fishing because he wants a place, a foundation from which to assert his equal rights as a global citizen, even if home is a nuclear-contaminated island. He views life on Ebeye as a temporary home and works for the United States as a matter of survival, producing a bicultural existence that accepts the limitations of a Western worldview embodied by the American culture on Kwajalein, as well as the limits of life on the rural atolls. In this regard, Jebro recognizes the limits of any government to give him what he needs because industrial society itself fails to provide the essential sustenance for human survival—a sustenance which he finds at sea when he fishes. Ultimately, the hope for a redemptive return to homelands is tempered by the realization that home will remain transient, limbic. The terramarine environment thus challenges the protagonist to reinvent a way of life and identity situated within the "pull" of two cultures.

The anticolonial and antiempire sentiment of the novel is woven into a mythic drama in the carnivalesque actions of Etao and Noniep to emphasize the perspective that although the characters feel a dichotomous tension between colonized and imperial societies, there are alternative modes of knowledge and existence that help one perceive a way out of the dualisms of colonizer and colonized. The oppressive neocolonial environment creates the need for a new, modern consciousness that can challenge and overcome the discriminatory colonial order. Frantz Fanon suggests such a move by the colonized in *The Wretched of the Earth,* indicating that a new consciousness must incorporate native customs and history as well as contemporary values and behaviors, which are expressed here in the image of riding the nose of the shark.

Moreover, the new or modern consciousness in Barclay's novel is depicted in the ritual mythic actions of the mythical characters Noniep and Etao. Before the final battle that Noniep must face, he has a feast with Etao, who takes nose-dives from the sky to earth on U.S. missiles just for fun. Noniep is less powerful but more serious than Etao and eventually dies at the end in order to protect the Marshallese souls, especially those of the youth who have died. Before Noniep's final encounter with Wullep and his demons, he drinks beer with Etao and talks about beauty. Etao responds that Kareem Abdul Jabbar's skyhook is beautiful while Noniep describes the "different moods of daylight" (140). In this scene Noniep tries to convince Etao of the seriousness of the battle they face against evil, but Etao elides any commitment. As the demons approach to kill Noniep, Etao yells "Barf time!" because he ate and drank too much. Etao is a figure who straddles the dualism of good and evil by hovering around, not always engaging in the battle, but leaning more to help Noneip as a purveyor of positive forces.

Perhaps the father most painfully experiences and expresses the cultural conflicts established in the novel, suggesting that a cathartic social crisis pushes one to enact alternative modes of agency and identity. The current foreign domination by the government that caused the nuclear contamination of rural atolls and ensuing displacement creates a binding tension between two worlds or ways of life—that of the modern, industrial-military power of the United States versus that of the indigenous, terramarine livelihood on the rural atolls. When the boys leave to fish near Tar-Woj, Rujen wonders if his sons "would be able to endure the pull of two very different ways of living, and if he could not, which would he choose—if he had any choice at all" (25). This telling comment also applies to Rujen, who struggles to work and live within the American and Marshallese cultures. The pull between two worlds becomes a problem for Rujen, who feels caught between an American military-industrial paradigm and a local indigenous one that asserts a sovereign identity based on the idea of a geocultural right to equally inhabit a landscape overtaken by an imperial power.

Pressured to practice the Christian religion as an integral part of the American culture on Kwajalein where he works, Rujen joins a Catholic church and offers his volunteer service as a sign of a full conversion to and acceptance of American values. However, when two dolphins swim into the lagoon, Rujen's continual questioning of his own cultural allegiances between the Americans, who want to save the dolphins (and return them to the ocean), and the Marshallese, who view the trapped dolphins as a gift from the ocean (and want to kill them for food), is brought to a critical tension at work. He explains to his American boss at the sewage plant: "Marshallese don't go looking for dolphins, chasing them in the ocean, but it's a Marshallese custom that when you see a dolphin come inside the lagoon, that's a gift. No *negotiations* can change this" (120). Rujen defends the rights of the Marshallese, even though he has distanced himself from this culture and does not see the importance of the islanders' political protests for land rights, equal pay, and medical treatment.

Rujen is a man who has internalized American comments that Marshallese are "filthy" and "ignorant" to the point that he idealizes American culture and admires his supervisors at the military missile base (117–18). Nonetheless, Rujen finds himself defending the rights of the Marshallese on the dolphin issue, to such an extent that after he experiences a public humiliation that leads to an acute personal insight at church, he decides to butcher the dolphins and bring the meat back to the people on Ebeye. On this Good Friday at church, populated exclusively by white Americans, he is forced to walk the aisles with a basket to collect donations for the Americans to "Save the Dolphins" (200). His inner conflict reaches its highest intensity when he notices that the red cloth covering the figure of Jesus on the wooden crucifix has fallen off-center. He jumps to straighten the cloth, but realizes in midair that the wooden idol is termite-ridden. As it falls upon him, the head breaks off and the crown of thorns stabs his palm, drawing blood. At this moment, Rujen catches the head and looks into the eyes of the holy figure when both the object and his body land on the floor: "[b]etween the initial shock of the trauma to his hand and the onslaught of pain, just before the full horror of what he had done consumed him . . . the only thought in Rujen's head . . . was that the downcast eyes of Jesus Christ staring back at him, almond-shaped, deep dark brown . . . were in fact the eyes of a fellow Marshallese" (205). The Americans scream in outrage and Rujen believes they see him as the antichrist or Satan. Yet, he is presented as a Christ-like figure with the punctured and bleeding palm and the sacred red cloth floating down to cover Rujen's feet as he lays upon the ground with the head of Jesus in his hands.

The acknowledgment of sameness between himself and the "white" or Western godhead is a freeing moment that allows Rujen to realize that the catholicism of that island church was a deceitful practice that aimed to take people's money, not save their souls from hell. The termite-infested idol symbolizes the inadequacy and hollowness of a foreign religion to serve the Marshallese. More importantly, the scene demonstrates the ineptness of a religion to practice its own doctrines of justice, equality, and compassion. Rujen's effort to believe in this religion, based partly on its offer of salvation and the possibility of equality, and based partly upon his desire to be accepted and to succeed in the dominant culture, abruptly stops after his awareness that all religions seek a similar truth, serve a similar purpose for any human life, and that an unquestioning following of the oppressor's religion is dangerous.

After Rujen's recognition of a root humanity and shared equality between himself and Americans, between Marshallese indigenous worldviews/spirituality and that of a Western monotheistic Christianity, he performs an act that asserts his right to inhabit the islands, both Kwajalein and Ebeye, on his own terms and as a Marshallese by ceremonially killing the dolphins and transporting the meat to Ebeye. The protagonist's actions demonstrate that the tension or "pull" between two cultures, one the oppressor and the other the oppressed, creates an implausible bicultural existence that, rather than causing an inner destruction of the self, produces instead an expanding identification of the self with the geophysical place of existence and the ancestral lineage. This includes the customs that have been formed out of dwelling in a particular place, to the extent that individual identity moves beyond simply a resistance to the dominant foreign culture.

Rujen's son grapples with a conflict as well, but with graver consequences. When Jebro and Nuke camp at Tar-Woj, they are unaware that this island is home to the dwarf-sorcerer Noniep who sits beneath an expansive breadfruit tree (the same tree where Rujen's father died in an act of political protest against the U.S. nuclear bomb testing), recounting the history of the islands and its peoples to the tree. Noniep's spiritual power is channeled into Tar-Woj by imbuing the island with ancestral wisdom, creating that place as a refuge for ancestral wisdom. The dwarf's chants also function to protect the Marshallese and especially the two boys from harm: "[Noniep] sits on a sitting mat, chanting knowledge into an extraordinarily tall breadfruit tree. Webs of bright orange kaonon vines drape over him as a protection against demons" (84). The idea that in inhabiting a landscape one comes into contact with history or ancient cultural knowledge is depicted through Noniep, who tells stories for the preservation of humanity and the cosmic order. How the past is remembered and retold by Noniep and later transmitted to the boys helps to define not only Marshallese history, but that of the modern human condition.

However, the notion found in the novel that identity is shaped by a remembered relationship to the land and terramarine environment does not represent a blinding nationalism as an avenue to show a colonial or postcolonial fight over land rights. Edward Said argues that "The slow and often bitterly disputed recovery of geographical territory which is at the heart of decolonization is preceded—as empire had been—by the charting of a cultural territory . . . and ideological resistance" (208). Barclay's postnuclear novel articulates a similar concern regarding the demarcation of a cultural territory by a postcolonial people, but his novel adds a twist. Regarding the struggle for an ideological independence from imperial dominance, the novel raises different questions and concerns that mark a rhetorical trend in turn-of-the-century fiction that establishes a neocolonial, capitalistic discourse of empire.[15]

The terramarine environment, as a geopolitical territory, remains under dispute by the Marshallese and the U.S. government because the Marshallese government depends upon the United States to clean up the radiological contamination and provide money to address current and future health problems. However, total "decolonization" and sovereignty are apparently not desirable for the Marshallese government, since the United States protects and provides trust funds and financial assistance for the Marshallese, who have been relocated several times already in the world of the novel and historically. How, then, does one chart a territory when the territory does not exist, or when it is too polluted to inhabit? Does the recovery of contaminated lands constitute a reclamation of territory and a viable assertion of a modern political identity? The Marshallese in the novel cannot regain this loss of land. Even though an ideological resistance is possible, as exemplified in Jebro's musings and Rujen's actions, a revolutionary ideological resistance to political oppression seems implausible for a people that depend on the imperial power for socioeconomic survival. The novel does not provide clear answers but suggests that even though regaining lost land is impossible and political sovereignty impractical, an imaginative inhabitation of polluted homelands is an active strategy of survival.[16]

The conflicted relationship between self, empire, and place is thrown into high relief during the brothers' boat accident. When Jebro and Nuke leave Tar-Woj to return to Ebeye, their small boat becomes swamped with seawater after being sprayed by another powerboat driven by American teenagers who are fishing the same waters. Jebro and Nuke bail water out of the boat, but the ocean waves are too strong and high. They capsize. After fighting to stay afloat amidst massive swells for hours, Nuke is pulled under the waves, which is also a result of the evil Wullep who sends two demons, Kwojenmeto and Monalapen, to kill the younger brother. The following passage describes the moment when the boys become separated:

> [Jebro] was then suddenly feeling very helpless because there
> was nothing he could do about the large crashing roller bear-
> ing down on his brother . . . the boiling foam almost blinding
> white in the new sunlight. . . . When he surfaced again . . .
> he saw only trails of foam like claw marks on the ocean. He
> shouted, looking in all directions, but all he got in reply was
> the sound of the wind and the water. . . . Death ruled the
> ocean. (214)

The ocean and its coral islands are home to the boys where they have land rights and a sense of sovereignty. However, even though the Pacific is viewed as a type of second self to Jebro, this very ocean betrays him by swallowing his brother. The ocean is therefore viewed as a nonhuman sphere in which death is one of many natural courses of life.

However, more than only a terrifying place of death, the ocean is an unknown region, not entirely good or entirely evil. This perspective reflects Jebro's view of his economic dependence upon the foreign American power that fluctuates between a beneficial and a repulsive relationship. After a long time of waiting, Jebro believes his brother has been drowned, even though he hopes to see him reappear: "He trembled, his pain of loss, like the sea, attacking him in waves; his guilt, jabbing at him, taunting him with all the different things he might have done, just little things, and Nuke would still be at his side" (233). A "protective spirit" in the form of an *ekjab* (frigate pelican) saves Nuke by hiding his heartbeat from the paddling demons eager to eat it: "Kwōjenmeto sees then . . . that the ekjab is not so impotent as he thought. It has hidden the boy from Monalapen, the sound of his heart suddenly muffled among the million other hearts beating within the sea" (221). On the one hand, the smallness and insignificance of human life is demonstrated here. On the other hand, the sense of interdependence between the human and nonhuman worlds is revealed. Protected by the supranatural and situated as simply another being in the earth's ecosystem, the younger brother surfaces alive but unconscious near Jebro. Eventually, the American boys who swamped the brothers' boat return to help them.

The older brother's experience of what he first views as a definitive loss (the death of his brother) and his guilt demonstrates the constellation of natural, social, and mythic factors that influence the portrayal of suffering. Importantly, the scene explores how an individual can inhabit a damaged landscape and what narratives are available to tell a story about suffering and survival. The natural and supranatural systems of life in the ocean and atolls commingle to fashion a sense of place in which individual identity is situated in relation to a culturally and geographically based experience of enduring and overcoming disaster and emotional pain. In this regard, place is the director of the plot's action, the choreographer of the dance that directs the significance of behavior and emotion in the narrative.

The novel maintains a skeptical and ironical view on industrial "progress" of human society based upon military dominance and nuclear weapons by suggesting through the supranatural storyline that nuclear weapons are small players on the larger stage of a reality that privileges natural and supranatural as the ultimate reckoning forces. As noted in the earlier example, Noniep appears in the form of the *ekjab* to save Nuke from drowning. Later Noniep decides to die in order to continue to fight the demons who seek to destroy humans, especially the Marshallese on Ebeye. However, it is Etao the trickster who finally intervenes to help protect Noniep because Noniep's ghost is not powerful enough to fight off the "hordes of demons" coming to suck his soul out (161). For Etao the battle of life and death and battles between good and evil are fun games, as fun as a basketball game: "[Etao] soars through the clouds like a god, boasting of his godhood high above the choppy Kwajalein lagoon. He has bug-eye goggles strapped to his face, white cotton wristbands on his wrists" (291). During the battle between Noniep and Wullep, Etao interferes by riding a ballistic missile aimed at a rural atoll in order to distract the demons and allow Noniep to protect the Marshallese: "Soon Etao will enter the game. . . . Etao catches one of the warheads and tucks the glowing oblong thing low by his waist. . . . He pivots left . . . rising with the warhead . . . for a strong one-footed leap. . . . 'Skyhook!' he shouts. He whoops and claps his hands to applaud his own superior skill" (292). Etao is dressed in the #33 NBA jersey of the legendary basketball player Kareem Abdul Jabbar who mastered the famous "skyhook" shot, epitomizing a popular youth sport's idol in the 1980s who performed phenomenal athletic feats.

Etao directs the warhead to kill the demon attempting to murder Noniep, but he helps Noniep for no apparent reason other than for "fun" because Etao appears to be unbiased in the struggle between good and evil. For the human characters in the novel, the ballistic "testing" on the rural atolls acts as a reminder of the ongoing destruction of habitats and homelands by a foreign power. Yet, for the supranatural character Etao, who acts above the human and mythic battles, he uses the objects of evil to perform "good" by helping Noniep and protecting the boys. Etao enters the "game" to tip the scales in favor of the positive forces, but he employs the very weaponry of evil that has created the suffering of human characters that Wullep and his demons feed from.

Through the perspective of Etao, the novel indicates that life in its largest sense includes human, ecological, and supranatural players. For Etao, life is a game in which meaning arises from momentary enjoyment gleaned from specific actions and experiences. Even horror, pain, and suffering are available for comedy and satire because these compose the game of life. Etao's views on life and his aerial perspective of the planet indicate that the natural world is not simply a place of horror or a place of hope, but another realm of action in which the human individual is one among many players manipulating the field of action.

Moreover, the scene suggests that although the bombs produced by human civilization appear to establish a human supremacy over nature, it is finally nature as a nonhuman sphere of action and place often inhabited by supranatural figures that exerts the final decision and winning "shot" regarding the outcome of humanity. The supranatural/mytho-logical characters in the novel function "above" the human drama, but are themselves forces of a Marshallese imaginative resistance to a governmental power that exploits and massively displaces people. Near the end of the novel, Noniep has allowed himself to die in order to "save his soul" from Wullep and looks across the water at Ebeye: "Noniep trains his reaching gaze onto the darkened slum of Ebeye, the demon blighted island he more aptly names Melal. . . . Into this Melal, this playground of demons, Noniep goes alone" (282–83).

The novel suggests that territorial reclamation will not free the protagonists from emotional anguish, but that an imaginative reinhabitation of polluted atolls may offer a method of reconfiguring a modern cultural identity. For each protagonist a traumatic experience can create the opportunity for an individual to relocate referents for identity that does not result in pathology or death. Traumatic experience and its remembrance are forces that propel new formulations of the self and one's relation to the land, ocean, community, and nation. Particularly for Rujen, the transformation of consciousness and reorientation toward society after his crisis allow him to enlarge his scope of personal autonomy. Painful experiences catalyze the characters to relocate referents of the self in both livable landscapes and mythic narratives that compose a new geography of home.

Conclusion

My aim in this book has been to widen the interpretive possibilities of literary trauma theory by introducing more models and approaches. However, I do not wish to argue that there is only one alternative theory that acts antithetically to the traditional model. Instead, I have suggested that another model is a pluralistic one that takes into account multiple theories, affording a greater emphasis on the contextual factors of trauma and the importance of place in fictional portrayals. As my discussion demonstrated, the heterogeneous representation of trauma in fiction requires an analysis that relies upon several different theories from psychology and literature as well as other disciplines to explain its expression. The use of psychological models provides the scholar with a specific set of interpretive tools to explain art and emotion, but one must remember that psychological theories originate to help people deal with feelings and behaviors, while literary theory focuses on texts and meanings in a philosophical exploration of knowledge and existence. In this regard, literary trauma theory must throw a wider net to catch the manifold representations of trauma in literature.

In the preceding pages I showed that careful considerations of how memory functions and the ways that a traumatic experience influences subjectivity and consciousness are central to building a comprehensive methodology for literary trauma theory. Memory is of special importance to the debate on trauma and its representability because the traditionalist claims regarding the muteness, contagiousness, and shattering aspects of trauma lead back to theories regarding the process of remembering. In addition, I suggested that observing the distinctions of traumatic experience and responses in fiction would help avoid a reductive methodology in literary trauma studies. Marking these distinctions allows a view of trauma beyond a pathological paradigm. Rather than narrowly focusing on the subject's fragmentation, a pluralistic model encourages the scholar to broadly explore the role of social factors and cultural contexts that influence the meaning of the experience. Attention to the social dimensions of traumatic experience through an analysis of landscape points toward the view that responses to trauma are as much socially conditioned as they are influenced by idiosyncratic personality traits. In one of its many functions, landscape imagery displays the emotional action of the plot and the interplay between self, place, and society, further specifying the value ascribed to the experience and the act of remembering.

In each chapter I demonstrated that trauma is a disruptive experience, yet one that propels the protagonist and the plot forward to contemplate new ways of knowing the self and world. Trauma in a novel can catalyze the reformulation of identity and the coherence of the self, rather than intrinsically acting to annihilate knowledge. A text may suggest that although trauma may assert a powerful role in changing perceptions, it is not the sole feature of the protagonist's persona. The model of reconstitution indicates that trauma is a part of the self, but not the defining element, which is a view that privileges the inner constituency of an adaptive consciousness that ultimately overcomes threats. Moreover, the protagonist may convey a traumatic response to an overwhelming experience in microcosmic and macrocosmic ways in order to represent the cultural impact of the event. In different modes, the texts included in this study as well as other novels by such American writers as Dorothy Allison, Russell Banks, Edwidge Danticat, Cormac McCarthy, Toni Morrison, and Kurt Vonnegut, among others, demonstrate that trauma is understood in relation to cultural models of the self and suffering provided in the world of the novel.

To emphasize the need to topple the godhead of trauma as unrepresentable or a "black hole" and its rhetorical figuration in literary scholarship today, I explored the diversity of representations in literature that articulate a number of meanings. My analysis emphasized that art in the form of literature represents trauma as located in specific people, bodies, and physical places in which the meaning of the experience is varied and uneven due to myriad factors, not transcendent factors, such as the contextual factors of place and landscapes. The traditional model of trauma in literary studies leads not only to a misrepresentation of the variable experiences and meanings derived from and produced by trauma in fiction, but also narrowly defines the process of remembering. Based on the traditional abreactive model of trauma, literary theorists tend to conflate significant distinctions between the protagonist's experience and remembrance of trauma. However, a pluralistic model suggests that how the person views the self before and after the traumatic event depends upon the type of traumatic event, as well as the available culturally informed narrative structures for expressing the experience that are made accessible through social values and practices in the world of the novel. Novels may show the discontinuity in the perception of self and reality as pathological as well as non-pathological. Trauma might be shown to disrupt the previous framework of reality that the protagonist functions within, causing the character to reorganize the self in relation to this new view of reality. This reordering is sometimes successful for characters or communities, but other times the protagonist cannot find relief or remedy. Novels may show that the traumatized protagonist is forced to reorganize perceptions of reality and the narrative examines how the event changed previous conceptions of the self. Importantly, the coping mechanisms are not universally portrayed as pathological in all novels or even within a single novel. The variety of traumatic representations in fiction conveys the view that traumatic responses and the social valuation of the experience can and do change over time. To consider that traumatic responses change over time means that individuals may respond differently to a similar experience of violence at different historical periods depending on the values of the society at that juncture in time.

A critical practice of analyzing trauma in literature should embrace pluralism in terms of the diverse range of theories on trauma and memory. A pluralistic model incorporates heterogeneity as its ideological reference point and as such extends beyond essentialist structures, especially in terms of conceptualizing the function and purpose of memory.

A particularly critical approach would excavate the concept of trauma, thus directing us to new questions such as: Can we imagine a traumatic experience or response beyond that of a disease or the unrepresentable? Is the pathological paradigm's etiology a process of othering what is not understood nor permitted within hegemonic frameworks? If one shifts the focus away from the "disease" of trauma and looks at the construction of the disease within society or cultural structures as depicted in a text, then another type of analysis unfolds. In discussing conceptualizations of psychological illness, Michel Foucault asks: "If this subjectivity of the insane is both a call to and an abandonment of the world, is it not of the world itself that we should ask the secret of its enigmatic status?" (56). This turn toward examining the contextual factors of traumatic responses and behaviors moves the emphasis away from the disease-oriented paradigm of the traditional model found in literary criticism.

Foucault's position regarding how one labels emotional responses and behaviors as "pathological" ties in with the critiques by contemporary psychologists of labeling responses as pathological, such as Derek-Summerfield, who points out the limits of Western psychiatric models to address experiences of war and atrocity that occur in countries outside the Western world:

> Psychiatric models like PTSD, even if the DSM-IV version brings improvements, have inherent limitations in capturing the complex ways in which individuals, communities, and indeed whole societies register massive trauma, socialize their grief, and reconstitute meaningful existence. Traumatic experience, and the search for meaning which it triggers, must be understood in terms of the relationship between the individual and his or her society, with outcomes influenced by cultural, social, and political forces which themselves evolve over time (27).

Summerfield emphasizes that although the experience has already occurred, how one relates to the experience shifts according to a variety of contextual factors. You cannot pull back the fist that punched you, but *how* you interpret it matters and this interpretation is malleable.

If we understand trauma in the novel beyond that of the pathological, then we enter another analytical dimension with different views. Trauma in fiction might even be interpreted as a form of tragedy that illuminates pain by situating experience within a larger cultural framework of action. This larger framework includes emotional signification that arises from contextual factors such as society, nature, myth, and ritual. Tragedy as defined by Aristotle in his *Poetics* contains "events inspiring fear or pity" that work together to produce a catharsis or purgation.[1] Friedrich Nietzsche, however, suggests that tragedy does not "purge" one of fear, but invites one to embrace the so-called unimaginable loss and celebrate oneself "beyond all horror and pity" (*Twilight of the Idols* 121). For Nietzsche, the "satyric chorus" of Dionysian tragedy situates the action of the human drama within the context of culture and nature so that "nature which has become estranged, hostile, or subjugated, celebrates once more her reconciliation with her prodigal son, [hu]man" (*Birth of Tragedy* 4).

In a Nietzschean model, tragedy provides a "metaphysical comfort" in the downfall or destruction of the individual in order to reinstate his or her "primordial unity" or "mystic oneness with the primal nature of the universe" (*Birth of Tragedy* 4, 5). To acknowledge extreme experience, loss, or death within a modern tragic/traumatic form would mean to consider that trauma is a possible part of human existence, thus eliding predetermined values of positivity or negativity.[2] If one considers trauma in contemporary novels as a type of tragedy, then trauma tragedy would be a genre in addition to the revenge tragedy, domestic tragedy, or tragicomedy.

Taking this broader approach, one finds that trauma tragedy or the ritual of suffering in the novel is situated in relation to a context-dependent signification that contains the representation of myth-rituals with its basis in nature. For example, in Cao's novel the betel nut myth (tied to a specific landscape) and karmic doctrines are linked to the representation of emotional pain and suicide. The myth-rituals of a hybridized indigenous healing ceremony and the ancient Native American petroglyph on a cave rooted in the southwestern landscape inform the depictions of loss and fear in Silko's novel. In Abbey's novel, the mythologies of European romance and an ecological (non-anthropocentric) worldview direct the portrayals of agony and lack of healing. In Barclay's *Melal*, an ecological mythology of supranatural characters and natural forces creates rituals for the performance of an identity linked to landscape, family, society, and the military. Moreover, the mythology of nationalism is an important component in each novel that informs the conceptualization of pain within individual and collective parameters.

In discussing the contextual factor of place in the depiction of trauma in the previous chapters, I especially addressed the ways that a place in nature expresses the value of a traumatic experience. To a certain extent, trauma in the novel can be seen to reveal the "horror and absurdity of existence" that Nietzsche describes as a function of tragedy (*Birth of Tragedy* 23). In the late-modern novels discussed here, it is the horror and absurdity of traumatic experience that demands a reconsideration of human existence. I addressed how the experience of trauma in the novel informs identity and consciousness through a performance that is situated in relation to particular places and cultures.

The performance of trauma occurs through the medium of place, for the representation of place holds both the performance and projection of values. In Cao's novel, the absurd and terrifying aspects of existence are expressed by Thanh and her ambivalent relationship to the past, a relation which is tied to the tragic myth of the betel nut story and the natural environment of the Mekong Delta region with its rice fields and monkey bridges. Silko's novel demonstrates the annihilation of existential boundaries between the human, natural, and supernatural as the hero reconciles his individual existence with that of his community and mythological narratives of survival. The collapse of the individual into the "primordial unity" of "oneness" that Nietzsche locates in Dionysian tragedy is represented in the function of the traumatized protagonist who acts within individual and collective levels. Rather than annihilating knowledge, trauma in the novel reaffirms the contradictions of existence that situate human life within larger machinations of meaning and action in which the human is not the central actor. If viewed as a part of the tragic form, then trauma in the novel might even indicate that, in Nietzsche's words, "life is indestructibly powerful and pleasurable" (*Birth of Tragedy* 22). In Abbey's novel, a blend of the tragic and romance genres, it is precisely this flux of phenomena between internal and external worlds that lands the protagonist in a mystifying state of sorrow in which he questions his subjectivity and memory against the nonhuman nature of the desert canyon. The character's humanness or anthropocentric subjectivity dissolves into a natural universe where existence is governed by the search for water and the search for the terrible truth regarding the disappearance of his beloved. Abbey's character is lost in the "oneness" of nature with the knowledge of the absurdity of human life without redemption, therefore paradoxically reaffirming the human's role in the natural universe. Within Barclay's novel, the Keju family's past trauma and their current exposure to toxic pollution from a neocolonial empire produce an absurd existence that is paralleled by the tragic mythic action of the supernatural characters in a battle between good and evil. The natural and supranatural are epistemological sites that both express the human condition and serve to outline the distance between humans and nature. This wide array of traumatic imagery in fiction underscores the interstitial nature of emotional pain and the need for an equally sensitive literary theory.

NOTES

Introduction

1. See E. V. Walter, *Placeways: A Theory of the Human Environment* (Chapel Hill: University of North Carolina Press, 1988).

2. See Laurence Kirmayer, "Landscapes of Memory: Trauma, Narrative, and Dissociation," in *Tense Past: Cultural Essays in Trauma and Memory*, ed. Paul Antze and Michael Lambek (New York: Routledge, 1996), 180. See also Jane Tilman, "Does Trauma Cause Dissociative Pathology?" in *Dissociation: Clinical and Theoretical Perspectives*, ed. S. J. Lynn and J. W. Rhue (New York: Guilford, 1994), 41–62.

Chapter 1

1. Elaine Scarry's *The Body in Pain: The Making and Unmaking of the World* (New York: Oxford University Press, 1985), can be viewed as a precursor to literary criticism on trauma. See also Ronald Granofsky, *The Trauma Novel: Contemporary Symbolic Depictions of Collective Disaster* (New York: Peter Lang, 1995).

2. For comprehensive overviews of the psychological concept of trauma, see Paul Lerner and Mark Micale, *Traumatic Pasts: History, Psychiatry, and Trauma in the Modern Age, 1870–1930* (New York: Cambridge University Press, 2001), 12. See also Ruth Leys, *Trauma: A Genealogy* (Chicago: University of Chicago Press, 2000), 120.

3. See Ronnie Janoff-Bulman, "The Aftermath of Victimization: Rebuilding Shattered Assumptions," in *Trauma and Its Wake*, ed. C. Figley (New York: Brunner-Mazel, 1985), 15–35.

4. See Colin Ross, *The Trauma Model: A Solution to the Problem of Comorbidity in Psychiatry* (Richardson: Manitou Communications, 2000). See also John Freedy and John Donkervoet, "Traumatic Stress: An Overview of the Field," in *Traumatic Stress: From Theory to Practice* (New York: Plenum, 1995), 3–28; Thomas Scheff, *Emotions, The Social Bond, and Human Reality: Part/Whole Analysis* (Cambridge, Eng.: Cambridge University Press, 1997); Paul Wachtel, "The Contextual Self," in *Trauma and Self*, ed. Charles Strozier and Michael Flynn (London: Rowman and Littlefield, 1996), 45–

56; Linda Williams and Victoria Banyard, *Trauma and Memory* (Thousand Oaks, Calif.: Sage, 1999), 57–67.

5. See American Psychiatric Association, *Diagnostic and Statistical Manual of Mental Disorders, Fourth Edition* (Washington, D.C.: American Psychiatric Association, 2000), 425. See also Marlene Steinberg, *Handbook for the Assessment of Dissociation: A Clinical Guide* (Washington, D.C.: American Psychiatric Press, 1995); Jennifer Freyd and Anne DePrince, "The Harm of Trauma: Pathological Fear, Shattered Assumptions, or Betrayal?" in *Loss of the Assumptive World: A Theory of Traumatic Loss*, ed. J. Kauffman (New York: Brunner-Routledge, 2002), 71–82; David Becker, "The Deficiency of the Concept of Posttraumatic Stress Disorder When Dealing with Victims of Human Rights Violations," in *Beyond Trauma: Cultural and Societal Dynamics*, ed. Rolf Kleber, Charles Figley, and Berthold Gersons (New York: Plenum, 1995), 99–110.

6. Regarding publications on trauma in disciplines outside of literature and psychology that articulate this view, see Ron Eyerman, *Cultural Trauma* (Cambridge, Eng.: Cambridge University Press, 2001). Eyerman upholds the traditional trauma model to assert that cultural trauma "refers to a dramatic loss of identity and meaning, a tear in the social fabric, affecting a group of people" (2). See also Jeffrey Alexander, "Toward a Theory of Cultural Trauma," in *Cultural Trauma and Collective Identity* (Berkeley: University of California Press, 2004). Alexander supports the traditional Freudian model and employs the shattering trope and rhetoric of pathology.

7. For the argument that reading a narrative can vicariously traumatize the reader, see Shoshana Felman and Dori Laub, *Testimony: Crises of Witnessing in Literature, Psychoanalysis, and History* (New York: Routledge, 1992).

8. For further discussions on essentialism, race, and racial identity, see Paul Gilroy, *Against Race* (Cambridge, Mass.: Belknap, 2000). See also Samira Kawash, *Dislocating the Color Line* (Stanford, Calif.: Stanford University Press, 1997); and Paul Outka, *Race and Nature* (New York: Palgrave Macmillan, 2008). For a critique of othering and pathologizing of Africa and African identity in Western philosophical traditions and discourses, see Achille Mbembe, *On the Postcolony* (Berkeley: University of California Press, 2001). Mbembe argues that "the African human experience constantly appears in the discourse of our times as an experience that can only be understood through a *negative interpretation*" (1).

9. See Lisa Butler and Oxana Palesh, "Spellbound: Dissociation in the Movies," *Journal of Trauma and Dissociation* 5, no. 2 (2004): 61–87. See also Anne DePrince and Jennifer Freyd, "Dissociative Tendencies, Attention, and Memory," *Psychological Science* 10, no. 5 (1999): 449.

10. For a further discussion on identity, race, and emotional suffering,

see Anne Cheng, *The Melancholy of Race* (Oxford: Oxford University Press, 2000). Cheng argues that "the social and subjective formations of so-called racialized or minority subjects are intimately tied to the [psychological] experience of grief" (x).

11. To explore further the interaction between reader and text, see Richard Gerrig, *Experiencing Narrative Worlds: On the Psychological Activities of Reading* (New Haven, Conn.: Yale University Press, 1993). Gerrig argues that "readers must use their own experiences of the world to bridge gaps in the text. They must bring both facts and emotions to bear on the construction of the world in the text" (17).

12. For other examples of the traditional model found in literary publications, see Deborah Horvitz, *Literary Trauma: Sadism, Memory, and Sexual Violence in American Women's Fiction* (Albany: State University of New York Press, 2000). Horovitz touches upon a common paradox that the traditional model emphasizes: "how to live in the present without cancelling a painful past" (166). See also how Anne Whitehead stresses the contradiction of trauma in *Trauma Fiction* (Edinburgh: Edinburgh University Press, 2004). See also J. Brooks Bouson, *Quiet as It's Kept* (Albany: State University of New York Press, 2000).

13. For an extensive examination regarding the theories, debates, research, and data on memory in the field of psychology, see Richard McNally's *Remembering Trauma* (Cambridge, Mass.: Belknap, 2003).

14. Ross distinguishes between intense retelling and abreaction, making clear that "intense retelling" (not abreaction) of the story of trauma to another person is "an essential component to recovery" (258). See Ross, *The Trauma Model*.

Chapter 2

1. See Linda Trinh Vo, "The Vietnamese American Experience: From Dispersion to the Development of Post-Refugee Communities," in *Asian American Studies,* ed. Jean Yu-wen Shen Wu and Min Song (New Brunswick, N.J.: Rutgers University Press, 2002), 291–92. Vo points out that there are two different groups of Vietnamese refugees: the 1975 evacuees and the "boat people." The 1975 evacuees assisted by the U.S. military were "a select group primarily from middle-class and elite backgrounds," and they spent a short period in "processing camps" before being relocated with three years' monetary assistance (291). Thanh represents this first group of refugees who left Saigon in April 1975. When Thanh leaves she first stays for four months in Fort Chaffee, an army camp used as a "refugee resettlement center" in Arkansas, before she joins her daughter in Virginia (30). In contrast, in 1978–80 there was a massive exodus of refugees who made perilous jour-

neys in boats across dangerous seas to spend long periods in refugee camps before being relocated in the United States. Regarding the significance of ethnic communities for the immigrant's survival in American, Vo writes: "The formation and maintenance of these ethnic enclaves defies the assimilationist theories, which suggest that the longer the immigrants are here, the more Americanized they will become. Some consider these communities as ethnic enclaves that will marginalize the ethnic groups and prevent full participation in American society; others see these ethnic clusters as a resource" (300).

2. For a further discussion on cultural identity and Asian American characters in fiction, see Stephen Sumida, "The More Things Change: Paradigm Shifts in Asian American Studies," *American Studies International* 38, no. 2 (2000): 92–120. Sumida argues that the representation of Asian Americans in fiction as having a dual identity is an "essentialist way of thinking about 'the East' and 'the West'" and marginalizes the Asian American figure by suggesting the character cannot find a home in either the East or West (112). In Cao's novel, the relationship between native and adopted nations, as well as past and present, is a non-hierarchical and multiply informed interaction determined by many factors including individual experience, community, and political climate.

3. For more discussion on cultural alienation, see Shen-mei Ma, *Immigrant Subjectivities in Asian American and Asian Diaspora Literature* (Albany: State University of New York Press, 1998). Ma charts the rhetorical strategies Asian American writers employ to represent an Asian immigrant subjectivity in literature. One method is to demonstrate how "cultural alienation" pathologically divides the subject and creates a schizophrenic immigrant character. These representations, for Ma, ultimately work to depict an active subjectivity. For a further discussion on the representations of Asian American subjects, assimilation, and "racial melancholia," see David Eng and Shinhee Han, "A Dialogue on Racial Melancholia," in *Loss: The Politics of Mourning*, ed. David Eng and David Kazanjian (Berkeley: University of California Press, 2003), 343–72.

4. For further discussion on the ambivalence of the relation to the American landscape for Asian Americans, see Cynthia Wong, *Reading Asian American Literature: From Necessity to Extravagance* (Princeton, N.J.: Princeton University Press, 1993). Wong argues that Asian immigrants and citizens viewed their relationship to the American landscape as highly ambivalent due to the racist policies of the imperial nation. According to Wong, relation to the American landscape for Euro-Americans represents unlimited possibility and imperial desire, while for Asian Americans the relation to the American landscape is a reminder of a lost home and a lack of lib-

erties due to anti-immigrant and anti-Asian legislation that, for example, excluded Asian immigrants from citizenship and owning land until the mid-twentieth century (123).

Chapter 3

1. Regarding the relation between identity, disease, perception, and landscape depicted in Native American literature, see Robert Nelson, *Place and Vision* (New York: Peter Lang, 1993). Susan Scarberry alludes to the text's place in the "literature of illness"; see Susan Scarberry, "Memory as Medicine," *American Indian Quarterly* 5, no. 1 (February 1979): 63–70. G. Thomas Couser examines how memory, especially "collective memory," functions as a mode of storytelling to connect Tayo to the land and community so that his healing depends on an "active re-creation" and recognition of his past (114); see G. Thomas Couser, "Oppression and Repression: Personal and Collective Memory in Paule Marshall's *Praisesong for the Widow* and Leslie Silko's *Ceremony*," in *Memory and Cultural Politics: New Approaches to American Ethnic Literature*, ed. Amritjit Singh and Joseph Skerrett (Boston: Northeastern University Press, 1996), 106–21. See also Edith Swann, "Laguna Symbolic Geography and Silko's *Ceremony*," *American Indian Quarterly* 12, no. 3 (1988): 229–49.

2. Regarding the subject of colonization, displacement, and Native American identity, see Louis Owens, *Other Destinies: Understanding the American Indian Novel* (Norman: University of Oklahoma Press, 1992). For a discussion on Native American writers' depiction of the relationship between Native Americans and the land, in terms of an ecological land ethic articulated through a Native American cultural perspective, see Lee Schweninger's *Listening to the Land* (Athens: University of Georgia Press, 2008).

3. For a further discussion on the significance of colonization in Native American literature and the ways that literary critics address the issue, see Arnold Krupat, *Red Matters* (Philadelphia: University of Pennsylvania Press, 2002). Krupat argues: "It seems to me that so far as any critical account of Native American literature would be anticolonial in its possible effect, that account at this historical juncture must acknowledge and legitimate invocations of the nation in opposition to oppression" (7).

4. For more discussion on the significance of objects in Navajo sandpainting ceremonies, see Valerie Harvey, "Navajo Sandpainting in *Ceremony*," in *Critical Perspectives on Native American Fiction*, ed. Richard Fleck (Philadelphia: Three Continents, 1993), 293–300.

5. See Tom Lynch, *Xerophilia* (Lubbock: Texas Tech University Press, 2008).

6. For a discussion on the problematic cultural assumptions of identity as defined by racial purity or blood quantities, see Lindsey Smith, *Indians,*

Environment, and Identity on the Borders of American Literature (New York: Palgrave Macmillan, 2008). Smith argues that novels by Native American writers such as Silko "complicate the language of 'blood'" in conceptualizations of racial identity" (4).

Chapter 4

1. See Richard Tottel, *Tottel's Miscellany* (1557), ed. H. Rollins (Cambridge, Mass.: Harvard University Press, 1928).

2. The sentence "Monarch of the moment" alludes to Henry Thoreau's *Walden* in which he quotes a poem by William Cowper. See Henry Thoreau, *Walden* (1854; Boston: Beacon, 1997), 44.

3. For a further discussion on symbolic geography, see Edward Muir and Ronald Weissman, "Social and Symbolic Places in Renaissance Venice and Florence," in *The Power of Place: Bringing Together Geographical and Sociological Imaginations*, ed. John Agnew and James Duncan (Boston: Unwin Hyman, 1989), 82.

Chapter 5

1. Karen Till, "Recent Projects," *The New Berlin: Memory, Politics, and Place*, http://www.geog.umn.edu/people/till/index.html.

2. For a further discussion on Western imperialism and the formation of U.S. cultures within such contexts as European colonization, slavery, westward expansion, overseas intervention, and cold war nuclear power, see Amy Kaplan, *Cultures of U.S. Imperialism* (Durham, N.C.: Duke University Press, 1993). See also Michael Hardt and Antonio Negri, *Empire* (Cambridge, Mass.: Harvard University Press, 2000).

3. Primarily Marshallese people were killed and injured, but also U.S. soldiers and Japanese fishermen on board a Japanese fishing vessel in the specific case of the Castle Bravo atomic bomb test became sick and died from the radiologic exposure to this bomb. See *Radio Bikini*, dir. Robert Stone, Cast: Kilon Bauno and John Smitherman as themselves (Robert Stone Productions, 1988). See also Neal O. Hines, *Proving Ground: An Account of the Radiobiological Studies in the Pacific, 1946–1961* (Seattle: University of Washington Press, 1962).

4. See "Operation Castle 1954 Pacific Proving Ground," May 17, 2006, http://nuclearweaponarchive.org/Usa/Tests/Castle.html.

5. See Richard Rhodes, *Dark Sun: The Making of the Hydrogen Bomb* (New York: Simon and Schuster, 1995).

6. See E. P. Cronkite, R. A. Conard, and V. P. Bond, "Historical Events Associated with Fallout from Bravo Shot-Operation Castle and 25 Y of Medical Findings," *Health Physics* 73 (1997): 176–86.

7. The United States medical study was called "Project 4.1 Study of Response of Human Beings Exposed to Significant Beta and Gamma Radiation due to Fall-Out from High Yield Weapons," March 6, 1954. See E. P. Cronkite et al., "Study of Response of Human Beings Accidentally Exposed to Significant Fallout Radiation, Operation CASTLE—Final Report Project 4.1," Naval Medical Research Institute, Naval Radiological Defense Laboratory, Defense Atomic Support Agency, Oak Ridge National Laboratory, Report #WT-923 (October 1954).

8. See United States, "Summary of Thyroid Findings in Marshallese 22 Years After Exposure to Radioactive Fallout" (Upton, N.Y.: Brookhaven National Laboratory, 1977). See Phillip Muller, "Statement of the Government of the Marshall Islands to the Senate Energy and Natural Resources Committee" (Washington, D.C., June 26, 1996).

9. See "Collateral Damage," *Unnatural Causes: Is Inequality Making Us Sick?* dir. Eric Stange. California Newsreel, 2008. See also Giff Johnson, "Pacific Islands Report," April 16, 2004, http://166.122.164.43/archive/2004/April/04-16-17.htm.

10. The Compact of Free Association includes an espousal provision, prohibiting Marshall Islanders from seeking future legal redress in U.S. courts and dismissing all current court cases in exchange for a $150 million compensation trust fund. See "Nuclear Testing in the Marshall Islands: A Chronology of Events," in *Nuclear Testing in the Marshall Islands: A Brief History* (Majuro: Micronitor News and Printing Company, August 1996). Under the amended compact, the U.S. will provide the Marshall Islands with financial assistance every year until 2023, including contributions to a jointly managed trust fund. See U.S. Department of State, "Background Note: Marshall Islands," January 1, 2009, http://www.state.gov/r/pa/ei/bgn/26551.htm. Information also gathered from the online database of the U.S. Dept. of Commerce STAT-USA/Internet, which is no longer available.

11. See David Gegeo, "Cultural Rupture and Indigeneity: The Challenge of (Re)visioning 'Place' in the Pacific, *The Contemporary Pacific*, 13, no. 2 (Fall 2001): 491–507. For further discussion on the links between identity, imagination, and place, see also Anne Buttimer, "Home, Reach, and Sense of Place," in *The Human Experience of Space and Place*, ed. Anne Buttimer and David Seamon (New York: St. Martin's, 1980).

12. For an extended examination of interrelationships between power, politics, identity, place, and the poor, especially in terms of the limited civic rights of poor and marginalized peoples in the postcolonial world, see Partha Chatterjee's writing on this subject in *The Politics of the Governed: Reflections of Popular Politics in Most of the World* (New York: Columbia University Press, 2006). For a further discussion on the relations between local, na-

tional, and global identities in connection with cultural, political, and spiritual investments in a "sense of place," specifically in terms of environmental literature, see Ursula Heise, *Sense of Place and Sense of Planet* (Oxford: Oxford University Press, 2008).

13. See Homi Bhabha, "Difference, Discrimination, and the Discourse of Colonialism," in *The Politics of Theory*, ed. Francis Barker, Peter Hulme, Margaret Iverson, and Diana Loxley (Colchester: University of Essex Press, 1983), 194–211. See also Ania Loomba, *Colonialism/Postcolonialism* (London: Routledge, 1998).

14. For a further discussion on the Pacific Rim as region and as a source of U.S. geopolitical identity, specifically in relation to the cold war years and the Soviet socialist bloc, see Christopher Connery, "Pacific Rim Discourse: The U.S. Global Imaginary in the Late Cold War Years," in *Asia/Pacific as Space of Cultural Production* (Durham, N.C.: Duke University Press, 1995), 30–57. For a discussion regarding "contradictory subjects" produced within the imperial language and cultural institutions of the empire, see Lisa Lowe, *Immigrant Acts: On Asian American Cultural Politics* (Durham, N.C.: Duke University Press, 1996).

15. For a further discussion on empire as a global market and production circuits that create a global order and a form of sovereign power, see Michael Hardt and Antonio Negri, *Empire* (Cambridge, Mass.: Harvard University Press, 2000).

16. Regarding the tensions between viewing national and local identities as a repressive symbol of hegemony or a mechanism of resistance to colonialism, see Roxann Prazniak and Arif Dirlik, *Places and Politics in the Age of Globalization* (Lanham, Md.: Rowman and Littlefield, 2001).

Conclusion

1. *Tragoidia* means singer in a tragic chorus and is derived from *tragoidos*, which means (he-)goat song and may refer to the "sacrifice of a goat in the vegetation and fertility rituals associated with the god Dionysus" (Kuiper 1126). See Kathleen Kuiper, ed., *Merriam-Webster's Encyclopedia of Literature* (Springfield, Mass.: Merriam-Webster, 1995).

2. For a further discussion on loss and melancholia in literature and culture within a Freudian framework but that gestures beyond a pathological paradigm, see David Eng and David Kazanjian, *Loss: The Politics of Mourning* (Berkeley: University of California Press, 2003). Eng and Kazanjian argue: "Instead of imputing to loss a purely negative quality . . . [loss] is . . . productive rather than pathological, abundant rather than lacking, social rather than solipsistic" (ix).

WORKS CITED

Abbey, Edward. *Black Sun*. New York: Avon Books, 1971.

Abrams, M. H. *A Glossary of Literary Terms*. Chicago: Holt, Rinehart and Winston, 1988.

Agnew, John, and James Duncan, eds. *The Power of Place*. London: Unwin Hyman, 1989.

Alexander, Jeffrey. "Toward a Theory of Cultural Trauma." In *Cultural Trauma and Collective Identity*, ed. Jeffrey Alexander et al. Berkeley: University of California Press, 2004.

Alexander, Jeffrey, Bernhard Giesen, and Jason Mast. *Social Performance: Symbolic Action, Cultural Pragmatics, and Ritual*. Cambridge, Eng.: Cambridge University Press, 2006.

Allen, Paula Gunn. *The Sacred Hoop: Recovering the Feminine in American Indian Traditions*. Boston: Beacon, 1986.

American Psychiatric Association. *Diagnostic and Statistical Manual of Mental Disorders, 4th Edition*. Washington, D.C.: American Psychiatric Association, 2000.

Anderson, Benedict. *Imagined Communities: Reflections on the Origin and Spread of Nationalism*. London: Verso, 1991.

Barclay, Robert. *Melal: A Novel of the Pacific*. Honolulu: University of Hawaii Press, 2002.

Bartlett, Frederic C. *Remembering: A Study in Experimental and Social Psychology*. New York: Macmillan, 1932.

Basso, Keith. "'Speaking with Names': Language and Landscape Among the Western Apache." *Cultural Anthropology* 4, no. 4 (1989): 99–130.

Becker, David. "The Deficiency of the Concept of Posttraumatic Stress Disorder When Dealing with Victims of Human Rights Violations." In *Beyond Trauma: Cultural and Societal Dynamics*, ed. Rolf Kleber, Charles Figley, and Berthold Gersons, 99–110. New York: Plenum, 1995.

Berger, James. *After the End: Representations of Post-Apocalypse*. Minneapolis: University of Minnesota Press, 1999.

Bhabha, Homi. "Difference, Discrimination, and the Discourse of Colonialism." In *The Politics of Theory*, ed. Francis Barker, Peter Hulme, Margaret Iverson, and Diana Loxley, 194–211. Colchester: University of Essex Press, 1983.

Blevins, Jacob. "The Catullan Lyric and Anti-Petrarchism in Sir Thomas Wyatt." *Classical and Modern Literature* 19, no. 3 (1999): 279–85.

Bloom, Edward. *The Order of Fiction.* New York: Odyssey, 1964.

Bouson, J. Brooks. *Quiet as It's Kept.* Albany: State University of New York Press, 2000.

Brennan, Timothy. *At Home in the World.* Cambridge, Mass.: Harvard University Press, 1997.

Brent, Linda. "Incidents in the Life of a Slave Girl." 1861. In *The Classic Slave Narratives,* ed. Henry Louis Gates, Jr. New York: Penguin, 1987.

Breuer, Joseph, and Sigmund Freud. "Studies on Hysteria." 1893–95. In *The Standard Edition of the Complete Psychological Works of Sigmund Freud,* vol. 2. Trans. J. Strachey. London: Hogarth, 1955.

Buell, Lawrence. *The Future of Environmental Criticism.* Oxford: Blackwell, 2005.

Butler, Lisa, and Oxana Palesh. "Spellbound: Dissociation in the Movies." *Journal of Trauma and Dissociation* 5, no. 2 (2004): 61–87.

Buttimer, Anne. "Home, Reach, and Sense of Place." In *The Human Experience of Space and Place,* ed. Anne Buttimer and David Seamon. New York: St. Martin's, 1980.

Cao, Lan. *Monkey Bridge.* New York: Penguin, 1997.

Caruth, Cathy. *Unclaimed Experience: Trauma, Narrative, and History.* Baltimore: Johns Hopkins University Press, 1996.

Cary, Cecile Williamson. "Sexual Identity in 'They Flee From Me' and Other Poems by Sir Thomas Wyatt." *Assays* 4 (1987): 85–96.

Chatterjee, Partha. *The Politics of the Governed: Reflections of Popular Politics in Most of the World.* New York: Columbia University Press, 2006.

Cheng, Anne. *The Melancholy of Race.* Oxford: Oxford University Press, 2000.

"Collateral Damage." *Unnatural Causes: Is Inequality Making Us Sick?* Dir. Eric Stange. California Newsreel, 2008.

Connery, Christopher. "Pacific Rim Discourse: The U.S. Global Imaginary in the Late Cold War Years." In *Asia/Pacific as Space of Cultural Production,* ed. Rob Wilson and A. Dirlik, 30–57. Durham, N.C.: Duke University Press, 1995.

Cronkite, E. P., R. A. Conard, and V. P. Bond. "Historical Events Associated with Fallout from Bravo Shot-Operation Castle and 25 Y of Medical Findings." *Health Physics* 73 (1997): 176–86.

Culbertson, Roberta. "Embodied Memory, Transcendence, and Telling: Recounting Trauma, Re-establishing the Self." *New Literary History* 26, no. 1 (1995): 169–95.

DePrince, Anne, and Jennifer Freyd. "Dissociative Tendencies, Attention, and Memory." *Psychological Science* 10, no. 5 (2000): 449.

Eng, David, and Shinhee Han. "A Dialogue on Racial Melancholia." In *Loss: The Politics of Mourning*, ed. David Eng and David Kazanjian, 343–72. Berkeley: University of California Press, 2003.

Eng, David, and David Kazanjian, eds. *Loss: The Politics of Mourning*. Berkeley: University of California Press, 2003.

Eyerman, Ron. *Cultural Trauma*. Cambridge, Eng.: Cambridge University Press, 2001.

Fanon, Frantz. "Les Damnes de la Terre." Ed. Francois Maspero. *Cahiers Libres* 27–28 (1961): 9–26.

———. *The Wretched of the Earth*. Trans. Constance Farrington. New York: Grove, 1965.

Farrell, Kirby. *Post-Traumatic Culture: Inquiry and Interpretation in the Nineties*. Baltimore: Johns Hopkins University Press, 1998.

Fergusson, Francis. *Aristotle's Poetics*. Trans. S. H. Butcher. New York: Farrar, Straus, and Giroux, 1961.

Foucault, Michel. *Mental Illness and Psychology*. 1954. Berkeley: University of California Press, 1987.

Freedy, John, and John Donkervoet. "Traumatic Stress: An Overview of the Field." In *Traumatic Stress: From Theory to Practice*, 3–28. New York: Plenum, 1995.

Freud, Sigmund. 1953–74 [1920]. "Beyond the Pleasure Principle." In *The Standard Edition of the Complete Psychological Works of Sigmund Freud*. Trans. and ed. James Strachey. Vol. 18. London: Hogarth, 1955.

———. 1953–74 [1914]. "Remembering, Repeating, and Working Through." In *The Standard Edition of the Complete Psychological Works of Sigmund Freud*. Vol. 12. London: Hogarth, 1955.

Freyd, Jennifer, and Anne DePrince. "The Harm of Trauma: Pathological Fear, Shattered Assumptions, or Betrayal?" In *Loss of the Assumptive World: A Theory of Traumatic Loss*, ed. J. Kauffman, 71–82. New York: Brunner-Routledge, 2002.

Gegeo, David. "Cultural Rupture and Indigeneity: The Challenge of (Re)visioning 'Place' in the Pacific." *The Contemporary Pacific* 13, no. 2 (Fall 2001): 491–507.

Gerrig, Richard. *Experiencing Narrative Worlds: On the Psychological Activities of Reading*. New Haven, Conn.: Yale University Press, 1993.

Gilroy, Paul. *Against Race*. Cambridge, Mass.: Belknap, 2000.

Glissant, Edouard. *Caribbean Discourse: Selected Essays*. Charlottesville: University of Virginia Press, 1989.

Granofsky, Ronald. *The Trauma Novel: Contemporary Symbolic Depictions of Collective Disaster*. New York: Peter Lang, 1995.

Hall, Stuart. "Cultural Identity and Diaspora." In *Colonial Discourse and Post-Colonial Theory*, ed. Patrick Williams and Laura Chrisman, 392–403. New York: Columbia University Press, 1992.

Handley, George. "A Postcolonial Sense of Place and the Work of Derek Walcott." *ISLE* 6, no. 3 (Summer 2000): 1–23.

Hardt, Michael, and Antonio Negri. *Empire*. Cambridge, Mass.: Harvard University Press, 2000.

Hartman, Geoffrey. "On Traumatic Knowledge and Literary Studies." *New Literary History* 26, no. 3 (Summer 1995): 537–63.

Harvey, Valerie. "Navajo Sandpainting in *Ceremony*." In *Critical Perspectives on Native American Fiction*, ed. Richard Fleck, 293–300. Philadelphia: Three Continents, 1993.

Heise, Ursula. *Sense of Place and Sense of Planet*. Oxford: Oxford University Press, 2008.

Henke, Suzette. *Shattered Subjects: Trauma and Testimony in Women's Life-Writing*. New York: St. Martin's, 1998.

Herman, Judith. *Trauma and Recovery: The Aftermath of Violence—From Domestic Abuse To Political Terror*. New York: Basic Books, 1992.

Hines, Neal O. *Proving Ground: An Account of the Radiobiological Studies in the Pacific, 1946–1961*. Seattle: University of Washington Press, 1962.

Horvitz, Deborah. *Literary Trauma: Sadism, Memory, and Sexual Violence in American Women's Fiction*. Albany: State University of New York Press, 2000.

Hungerford, Amy. *The Holocaust of Texts: Genocide, Literature, and Personification*. Chicago: University of Chicago Press, 2003.

Janet, Pierre. *Psychological Healing: A Historical and Clinical Study*. 1919. Trans. E. Paul and C. Paul. New York: Macmillan, 1976.

Kaplan, Amy, and Donald Pease, eds. *Cultures of U.S. Imperialism*. Durham, N.C.: Duke University Press, 1993.

Kawash, Samira. *Dislocating the Color Line: Identity, Hybridity, and Singularity in African American Literature*. Stanford, Calif.: Stanford University Press, 1997.

Kay, Dennis. "Wyatt and Chaucer: *They Fle From Me* Revisited." *Huntington Library Quarterly* 47, no. 3 (1984): 211–25.

Kirmayer, Laurence. "Landscapes of Memory: Trauma, Narrative, and Dissociation." In *Tense Past: Cultural Essays in Trauma and Memory*, ed. Paul Antze and Michael Lambek, 173–98. New York: Routledge, 1996.

Kleber, Rolf, Charles Figley, and Berthold Gersons. *Beyond Trauma: Cultural and Societal Dynamics*. New York: Plenum, 1995.

Kowalewski, Michael. "Bioregional Perspectives in American Literature." In *Regionalism Reconsidered*, ed. David Jordan. New York: Garland, 1994.

Krupat, Arnold. *Red Matters*. Philadelphia: University of Pennsylvania Press, 2002.

Kuiper, Kathleen, ed. *Merriam-Webster's Encyclopedia of Literature*. Springfield, Mass.: Merriam-Webster, 1995.

LaCapra, Dominick. *Writing History, Writing Trauma*. Baltimore: Johns Hopkins University Press, 2001.

———. "Trauma, Absence, Loss." Critical Inquiry 25.4 (1999): 696–728.

Lang, William. "From Where We Are Standing: The Sense of Place and Environmental History." In *Northwest Lands, Northwest Peoples: Readings in Environmental History*, ed. Dale Goble and Paul Hirt, 79–95. Seattle: University of Washington Press, 1999.

Leys, Ruth. *Trauma: A Genealogy*. Chicago: University of Chicago Press, 2000.

Loomba, Ania. *Colonialism/Postcolonialism*. London: Routledge, 1998.

Lowe, Lisa. *Immigrant Acts: On Asian American Cultural Politics*. Durham, N.C.: Duke University Press, 1996.

Lynch, Tom. *Xerophilia*. Lubbock: Texas Tech University Press, 2008.

Ma, Shen-mei. *Immigrant Subjectivities in Asian American and Asian Diaspora Literature*. Albany: State University of New York Press, 1998.

Mandel, Naomi. *Against the Unspeakable*. Charlottesville: University of Virginia Press, 2006.

Marx, Leo. *The Machine in the Garden: Technology and the Pastoral Ideal in America*. New York: Oxford University Press, 1964.

Mason, Harold A. *Sir Thomas Wyatt: A Literary Portrait*. Bristol: Bristol Classical, 1987.

Mbembe, Achille. *On the Postcolony*. Berkeley: University of California Press, 2001.

McNally, Richard. *Remembering Trauma*. Cambridge, Mass.: Belknap, 2003.

Meinig, D. W. "Commentary." "Power and Place in the North American West" symposium. Seattle, November 5, 1994. Typescript, filed at the Center for the Study of the Pacific Northwest, University of Washington.

Micale, Mark, and Paul Lerner. *Traumatic Pasts: History, Psychiatry, and Trauma in the Modern Age, 1870-1930*. New York: Cambridge University Press, 2001.

Morrison, Toni. *Beloved*. New York: Penguin, 1987.

Muir, Edward, and Ronald Weissman. "Social and Symbolic Places in Renaissance Venice and Florence." In *The Power of Place: Bringing Together Geographical and Sociological Imaginations,* ed. John Agnew and James Duncan, 81–105. Boston: Unwin Hyman, 1989.

Muller, Phillip. "Statement of the Government of the Marshall Islands to the Senate Energy and Natural Resources Committee." Washington, D.C., June 26, 1996.

Najita, Susan. *Decolonizing Cultures in the Pacific.* New York: Routledge, 2006.

Nelson, Robert M. *Place and Vision: The Function of Landscape in Native American Fiction.* New York: Peter Lang, 1993.

Nietzsche, Friedrich. *The Birth of Tragedy.* 1871. Trans. Clifton P. Fadiman. New York: Dover, 1995.

———. *Twilight of the Idols.* 1889. Trans. R. J. Hollingdale. London: Penguin, 1968.

Outka, Paul. *Race and Nature from Transcendentalism to the Harlem Renaissance.* New York: Palgrave Macmillan, 2008.

Owens, Louis. *Other Destinies: Understanding the American Indian Novel.* Norman: University of Oklahoma Press, 1992.

Pease, Donald. "New Perspectives on U.S. Culture and Imperialism." In *Cultures of United States Imperialism,* ed. Amy Kaplan and D. Pease. Durham, N.C.: Duke University Press, 1993.

Piers, Craig. "Remembering Trauma: A Characterological Perspective." In *Trauma and Memory,* ed. Linda Williams and Victoria Banyard, 57–67. Thousand Oaks, Calif.: Sage, 1999.

Prazniak, Roxann, and Arif Dirlik. *Places and Politics in the Age of Globalization.* Lanham, Md.: Rowman and Littlefield, 2001.

Radio Bikini. Dir. Robert Stone. Cast: Kilon Bauno and John Smitherman as themselves. Robert Stone Productions, 1988.

Rhodes, Richard. *Dark Sun: The Making of the Hydrogen Bomb.* New York: Simon and Schuster, 1995.

Ross, Colin. *The Trauma Model: A Solution to the Problem of Comorbidity in Psychiatry.* Richardson: Manitou Communications, 2000.

Sadock, Benjamin, Virginia Sadock, and Pedro Ruiz. *Comprehensive Textbook of Psychiatry.* Philadelphia: Lippincott Williams and Wilkins, 2009.

Said, Edward. *Culture and Imperialism.* New York: Random House, 1993.

Scarry, Elaine. *The Body in Pain: The Making and Unmaking of the World.* New York: Oxford University Press, 1985.

Scheff, Thomas. *Emotions, the Social Bond, and Human Reality: Part/Whole Analysis.* Cambridge, Eng.: Cambridge University Press, 1997.

Schweninger, Lee. *Listening to the Land.* Athens: University of Georgia Press, 2008.

Shauffler, F. Marina. *Turning to Earth*. Charlottesville: University of Virginia Press, 2003.

Silko, Leslie Marmon. *Ceremony*. New York: Penguin Books, 1977.

———. "Landscape, History, and the Pueblo Imagination." In *The Ecocriticism Reader: Landmarks In Literary Ecology*, ed. Cheryll Glotfelty and Harold Fromm, 264–76. Athens: University of Georgia Press, 1996.

Skeat, W. W., ed. *The Complete Works of Geoffrey Chaucer*. Oxford: Clarendon, 1899.

Slotkin, Richard. *Gunfighter Nation: The Myth of the Frontier in Twentieth-Century America*. Norman: University of Oklahoma Press, 1992.

Smith, Lindsey. *Indians, Environment, and Identity on the Borders of American Literature*. New York: Palgrave Macmillan, 2008.

Steinberg, Marlene. *Handbook for the Assessment of Dissociation: A Clinical Guide*. Washington, D.C.: American Psychiatric, 1995.

Sumida, Stephen. "The More Things Change: Paradigm Shifts in Asian American Studies." *American Studies International* 38, no. 2 (2000): 92–120.

Summerfield, Derek. "Addressing Human Response to War and Atrocity: Major Challenges in Research and Practices and the Limitations of Western Psychiatric Models." In *Beyond Trauma: Cultural and Societal Dynamics*, ed. Rolf Kleber, Charles Figley, and Berthold Gersons, 17–29. New York: Plenum, 1995.

Swann, Edith. "Laguna Symbolic Geography and Silko's *Ceremony*." *American Indian Quarterly* 12, no. 3 (1988): 229–49.

Szalay, Krisztina. *The Obstinate Muse of Freedom: On the Poetry of Sir Thomas Wyatt*. Budapest: Akademiai Kiado, 2000.

Tal, Kali. *Worlds of Hurt: Reading the Literatures of Trauma*. New York: Cambridge University Press, 1996. 15.

Till, Karen. *The New Berlin: Memory, Politics, Place*. Minneapolis: University of Minnesota Press, 2005.

Tilman, Jane. "Does Trauma Cause Dissociative Pathology?" In *Dissociation: Clinical and Theoretical Perspectives*, ed. S. J. Lynn and J. W. Rhue, 41–62. New York: Guilford, 1994.

Tottel, Richard. *Tottel's Miscellany*. 1557. Ed. H. Rollins. Cambridge, Mass.: Harvard University Press, 1928.

Tuan, Yi-Fu. *Space and Place: The Perspective of Experience*. Minneapolis: University of Minnesota Press, 1977.

Tumarkin, Maria. *Traumascapes*. Melbourne: Melbourne University Press, 2005.

United States. "Project 4.1 Study of Response of Human Beings Exposed to Significant Beta and Gamma Radiation due to Fall-Out from High Yield Weapons," March 6, 1954.

———. "Summary of Thyroid Findings in Marshallese 22 Years After Exposure to Radioactive Fallout." Upton: Brookhaven National Laboratory, 1977.

U.S. Department of State. "Background Note: Marshall Islands." January 1, 2009. http://www.state.gov/r/pa/ei/bgn/26551.htm.

Van der Kolk, Bessel A., and Onno van der Hart. "The Intrusive Past: The Flexibility of Memory and the Engraving of Trauma." In *Trauma: Exploration in Memory*, ed. Cathy Caruth, 158–82. Baltimore: Johns Hopkins University Press, 1996.

Vickroy, Laurie. *Trauma and Survival in Contemporary Fiction*. Charlottesville: University of Virigina Press, 2002.

Vo, Linda Trinh. "The Vietnamese American Experience: From Dispersion to the Development of Post-Refugee Communities." In *Asian American Studies*, ed. Jean Yu-wen Shen Wu and Min Song. New Brunswick, N.J.: Rutgers University Press, 2002.

Wachtel, Paul. "The Contextual Self." In *Trauma and Self*, ed. Charles Strozier and Michael Flynn, 45–56. London: Rowman and Littlefield, 1996.

Walter, E. V. *Placeways: A Theory of the Human Environment*. Chapel Hill: University of North Carolina Press, 1988.

West, Rinda. *Out of the Shadow*. Charlottesville: University of Virginia Press, 2007.

White, Richard, and John Findlay, eds. *Power and Place*. Seattle: University of Washington Press, 1990.

Whitehead, Anne. *Trauma Fiction*. Edinburgh: Edinburgh University Press, 2004.

Williams, Linda, and Victoria Banyard. *Trauma and Memory*. Thousand Oaks, Calif.: Sage, 1999.

Wilson, Rob, and Arif Dirlik, eds. *Asia/Pacific as Space of Cultural Production*. Durham, N.C.: Duke University Press, 1995.

Wong, Cynthia Sau-ling. *Reading Asian American Literature: From Necessity to Extravagance*. Princeton, N.J.: Princeton University Press, 1993.

Wyatt, Sir Thomas. "They Flee From Me." In *English Sixteenth-Century Verse*, ed. Richard Sylvester, 138. New York: Norton, 1984.

Young, Allan. *The Harmony of Illusions: Inventing Post-Traumatic Stress Disorder*. Princeton, N.J.: Princeton University Press, 1995.

index

ABOUT THE AUTHOR

Michelle Balaev is a visiting assistant professor of English at Wake Forest University in North Carolina.